EPIPHANY WEATHER

Ann Tracy

SPUYTEN DUYVIL

New York City

Library of Congress Cataloging-in-Publication Data

Names: Tracy, Ann Blaisdell, author.
Title: Epiphany weather / Ann Tracy.
Description: New York City : Spuyten Duyvil, [2023]
Identifiers: LCCN 2023012937 | ISBN 9781959556190 (paperback)
Subjects: LCGFT: Novels.
Classification: LCC PS3570.R26 E65 2023 | DDC 813/.54--dc23/
eng/20230324
LC record available at https://lccn.loc.gov/2023012937

Thanks, Alexis

THE LORDS OF LANDS

Silas Bassett, retired professor of English, paced and fretted. It was mainstreaming day at Goldengroves, long dreaded, when the decency of A Wing's apartments for the retired but sane would be disrupted by new neighbors from the Groves' less cogent reaches. Who knew what hell in wheelchairs was poised to roll down the corridors of A Wing? Not its residents, certainly— they had been given no particulars. The trustees who had dreamed this up would sleep tonight in the peace of accomplishment, oh yes, while he, Silas, would lie awake to the howls of a human zoo. It was a judgment on him, perhaps, for the days when he had referred to adversarial colleagues as pissers and moaners; now his words would be made flesh and dwell among them.

Possible, of course, that A would be lucky. If the system, whatever it was, failed (and there were rumors of lotteries, of names drawn from hats), his new neighbors could be people like himself, from B, or people still recognizable as having once been like himself, from C. But, caught in the dread of D-Wingers, that was not what he expected: he imagined the blots of puree, like the vomit of small woodland creatures, on his neighbors' plates; the blank chipper eyes of second childhood; the shouting and stenches, the abdication of all propriety. "Oh God, oh God," Silas prayed in a terrified gabble, "please no incontinents, please no screamers. Send the blind if you must, Lord, send the cripples, provided they're serious minded. In the name of sweet organized Jesus, amen."

At least he was staying on A Wing himself. After a life of letter grades, A-Wingers could not help feeling that their place somehow reflected well on them, that moving even to equally rational B would signify demotion. He regretted his colleagues whom the great shuffle had sent into exile. The pair of ancient entomologists in the three-room, who wore ties even with their bathrobes, had murmured exclamations soft as the wings of moths —hoop-la, shoo-fly. Even the furious woman from Foreign Languages, a wheelchair psychopath who whizzed up behind the unwary and went for their knees, had been incontinent only in her rage, and the college was used to that; among strangers she would have been put in D wing at first sight. The fourth deportee, a bland professor of Art History who had been her favorite target, might in retrospect seem more desirable than they had known: he had at least been quiet.

Goldengroves offered partially subsidized refuge to all staff retired from the college that owned it, but in practice it was occupied mainly by professors. Employees of a more practical bent, secretaries in particular, had had a crawful of professors, as they enjoyed announcing, and not even the bargain rates made further contact worthwhile if they had any other option at all, including (as one of them remarked) a roofless bait shack in Florida. Retired administrators, though they had come from faculty ranks themselves, felt something similar; they wanted peace in old age, freedom from thread-bare quarrels and long-marinated academic resentments, freedom from fear of the vengeful cane hooked around the ankle. In any ordinary facility for the old, women outnumber men by four or five to one, but years of sexist hiring had produced at Goldengroves a preponderance of males, in whom the habits of testosterone, if not the stuff itself, showed signs of hanging on. The imbalance, however cruel its history, gave pleasure to many of the women who now lived with it and, for various reasons, to a number of the men as well.

Not everyone on A shared the misgivings of Silas Bassett. Orin Stanley, retired janitor, Stan the Jan to students, was looking forward to some real loonies. After his heart attack, he and Beth had sold up and moved into one of the three-rooms available to couples. From that front-row seat he reckoned to put his boots up and watch the pranks of decaying professors, who God knows had been funny enough when they had all their marbles. The new ones would likely make messes it was no longer his job to clean, and he'd watch that too. He'd liked his career at the college, especially when he could work in the classroom buildings—just as well to stay clear of the dorms— and especially the art building, where the semester's-end trash held some pretty good stuff—thrown-out pots to bring home for the garden, photos and drawings that looked okay to him. He liked the word "janitor" as well, none of those puffed-up names that made it sound like he'd never seen the business end of a broom; only Beth knew that his mother had raised him on Bullfinch's Mythology and that he still had the book. Plenty good enough for Doris Stanley's boy to be called after the god Janus.

Thatch Sinclair, Anthropology, was courting chaos too, though not in quite the same way. He had lately, out of profound boredom, been doing what he still thought of as a study about the reactions of the elderly westerner to Pacific Island sexual display. Once or twice a day, at unpredictable times, he would stroll down the corridor or pop out of a room, notebook in hand, penis exposed, to provoke a reaction, any reaction, anything oh god anything to break the monotony. So far Goldengroves had pretended so hard not to notice that he sometimes looked down to make sure he was still in one piece. He suspected that Silas at least was pained by the lack of decorum, but he had missed Orin's comment to Beth: "Whack it with a mop handle, I would." Thatch longed to do his trick for someone new, female would be good, unstable would not be bad. He hoped for chaos provoked by himself.

Herbert Christmas, retired College Chaplain, hoped most of all that the mixing of residents would not affect the catering. A testing ground for the college's Hotel and Restaurant Management Program, the A-Wing dining room had been blessed from time to time with duck a l' orange, roast pork stuffed with prunes, sole in white wine sauce. Student chefs loved making sauces, they felt professional with a whisk in their hands, and for this bit of innocent pride he applauded them. The critique of his dinners preempted the attention he had once given to questions of good and evil. His devotion had grown spindly, and now he feared that he loved God truly only while he was saying grace: Bless this food that you have given us and please keep it coming, amen. But it was his duty as a chaplain to greet the newcomers in a spirit of brotherly love, and to remember that any fallings off in the larder could not properly be blamed on them.

Sebastian Antioch, also retired from English but longer at Goldengroves than Silas, was at peace with the idea of new neighbors. He had for some time been withdrawing farther into silence, even at meals, keeping to himself and his books rather than visiting the lounge. This arose not from any dislike of his fellow creatures, but from his discovery that in moments of passion he compulsively repeated words or phrases, which made him sound more senile than he reckoned he was, as "You're out, you're out of your mind, out of your mind, asshole, asshole, out, you don't know your Shakespeare,

your Shakespeare, you damn fool damn you damn!"
He thought, with humor he could not share, that he
sounded like an oratorio, and he had never liked ora-
torios. Except for the rich linguistic flourishes of the
Tudor-Stewarts, he had always preferred economy of
language. From time to time he posted a quotation on
his door, a sign to the world that he was still alive and
lucid. He was aware without regret that Silas, whose
door faced his, did not care for his choices. Today he
had put up a stanza from Dante Gabriel Rossetti to hon-
or the new arrivals:

Piled deep below the screening apple-branch
They lie with bitter apples in their hands:
And some are only ancient bones that blanch,
And some had ships that last year's wind did launch,
And some were yesterday the lords of lands.

The blanching bones notwithstanding, he thought
that the memory of having yesterday been lords of
lands, even if the territories were intellectual, no, ES-
PECIALLY if the territories were intellectual, should be
some comfort, that it honored the substance of their

lives. He had been told in the past, by his nearest connections, that he had no knack for comforting, that not to make too fine a point of it, he was piss poor at that and should let it alone, but this was so contrary to his own perceptions that he paid it no mind. Beauty of all sorts was a comfort to him, and Rossetti's poem was beautiful. He hoped that the newcomers, however blanched, would feel welcome.

When at last A-Wing's new residents presented themselves, they proved to be all four of the deportees from C Wing, which Silas hoped, even in the midst of his tentative relief, would show the committee the incompetence of their process. True, the two singles appeared to be on the verge of D, but the couple looked like a bargain. Hand in hand and on their own four feet, Harlow and Millie Osgood were the first to arrive. Harlow, once Vice President for Continuing Education and not a bad sort if you could stand relentless cheer, had been on C since his stroke. The state of his wits could not be ascertained but his language had taken a hit, and he was inclined to choke in the dining room. The latter difficulty in particular had mandated C, and his A-Wing-quality wife had gone with him. "Cbrbodf!" he said to his old colleagues now, or something like it, and Millie said, "Yes, Harlow, I'm glad to see them too."

"What fun to be on A-Wing," Millie added, beaming. "The kitchens here are much better than those on C, you know. I'll get some real baking done now!"

Herbert Christmas, his eyes misty with gastronomical lust, caught both her hands in his. Beth was bouncing on her toes. She had missed the company of her own sex. "That Millie's a real woman," she said to Orin. "That Millie's a fucking saint," Orin said. He looked forward with pleasure to more of Harlow's conversation.

Behind the Osgoods, Glenda Fessette, retired librarian, wheeled herself with an overnight case on her lap. The transfer of the residents' possessions had been effected in off hours and had gone so smoothly, indeed, that it had evidently been left to work-study students, who were skilled at sudden moves.

Something lay behind Glenda's dreamy inscrutable face, but what it was none of the watchers could say. Under their gaze she shifted in her chair and the case slid from her lap, hit the floor, and popped open, though it was too neatly packed to spill more than her toothbrush in a baggie. "Mr. Jan," she said, having recognized something at last, "Mr. Stan, take care of this please."

Orin blew his nose. "I think Mr. Bassett will be helping you with your things," he said. Silas would get him for that, and for the Mr. too, but the trapped look in his eyes was worth it. Beside him Beth choked on a giggle. Silas had once come down on her for watching South Park in the lounge. There had been words about age-appropriate behavior and moral standards.

The fourth new neighbor was pushed by a nurse and wore a housecoat, not a good sign. Sebastian knew her. She had been a marine biologist. "Professor Hillman is feeling a little tired," said the nurse, "she'll be going down for a nap before she's ready to meet her new friends."

"Lily," said Sebastian carefully, "her first name is Lily." He had nearly said "was."

Lily and Millie, Orin thought, there's a treat. Get a damn goat and call it Billy.

Lily's new friends gave her a gingerly look. She appeared to be curdling into a heap like candle wax. And yet she came from C, they all told themselves, assisted living, she must be able to dress and feed herself.

"Lily," said Herbert Christmas, patting the shoulder of the housecoat, "sweet dreams, and we'll see you at supper."

Oh God, the others thought, so we will.

JANE AND OTHER PHANTOMS

Silas Bassett lay awake until four, listening in vain for the manic cries that would ruin his sleep. Supper had gone fairly well, thanks to Millie Osgood, who had gathered up the other new arrivals at one table, "just for tonight, till you get used to the new place," and taken care of them. Small sounds of choking and gagging had been audible but contained. Still angered by what might have been and what yet might be, Silas with some effort lay straight and quiet in his striped pajamas. Bed was a place of doubtful moral standing, things went on in beds, and he did not permit himself any untoward tossing and shifting. Instead of sheep he counted irritants old and new:

Confetti Noisemakers
Ferrets in little jackets
Casual sex and all the names for it
M & M's where chocolate chips should be
Rude jokes Split infinitives Limericks
Pre-sweetened cereal Stickers

Body piercing Mylar balloons
Imprecision in the use of "that" and "which"
Slapstick comedy
Neon-colored condoms

Here he grew agitated and forced his mind to thoughts more soothing. It was frivolity he abhorred in all its guises: foe to serious purpose, it thumbed its nose at agenda, it draped solemnity in streamers, it chuckled at the risqué. He fixed his mind on a world as sunlit and bare as a Shaker house, where men in low voices spoke nothing but sense. Clothed in white, they strolled between rows of shaped evergreens and agreed on goodness.

But when he fell at last into a restless doze, he dreamed not of his utopia but of Jane, his nemesis, the wife who had left him thirty years ago, to his everlasting profit. He dreamed not of her departure but, fearfully, of her return. She came, as always, on the wings of a storm—first the dark clouds smirching the sky, then the wind with its scraps of gaudy debris. Now, in his dream, he ran to his study for refuge, and there was Jane again, still young, barefoot perched on the edge of his desk, laughing.

"My papers!" he cried.

"What's on your papers, old man?" she teased, but he could utter no anatomical name for the part of her that was squashing his documents, though awake he knew a dozen terms, some of which he had never spoken aloud.

"Agendas!" he cried instead. "Class lists, bibliographies, resolutions!" "Yawn!" said Jane the Nightmare. "And when was the last time you dared to eat a peach?" As she left the room he snatched up his poor papers, now autumn leaves, small and crisp and brown. They were dust and shards in his fist, and Jane had done it, Jane the Witch. He covered his eyes and sobbed aloud.

She had never known what mattered.

Nightmares about Jane varied in their particulars but not in their theme: she had brought chaos and disruption to his ordered life. In the first year of their marriage she had served him a martini with a glass eye in lieu of an onion. She had meant it for a joke, but it had struck him with queasy foreboding. How had he married a woman who owned a glass eye as a toy? But Jane had a stash of odd bits, rubber body parts and bead rings, party poppers and rolls of ribbon, the means to make anything sillier than it had to be, as though frivolity was her life's mission. Why had he not left her first?

Across the corridor Sebastian was dreaming of Jane as well, as every night he hoped to do. By long habit he slept naked, his skin no longer taut but warm enough in the tropic indoor temperature of the Groves, his bathrobe at the ready. He'd been quite a boy in his day, he liked to think. He'd had Lily Hillman more than once on the smooth rocks of Schoodic Point, a bed not comfortable but picturesque with crashing waves; and if he could trust his memory, one of the old entomologists had had him in the field-house bleachers. Tip of the iceberg.

But Jane Bassett was the one true love of his life, his secret best friend and almost lover, who would surely have been his lover in the end, had she not broken and fled from Silas, disappeared into California, and that was the end of it all.

Sebastian had reckoned to marry in middle age, when he'd used up his wild oats, but he found to his dismay that after Jane no one else would do. It was not just the smell of her hair and the turn of her wrist, though those were clear to memory, but she had loved words as he did, lucid words, froufrou words, thundering black funereal words. She and she alone had seen with Sebastian that the Metaphysical poets not only (as all the 20th century knew) wedded intellect and passion, but that their very extravagance of language, as frivolous as death was deep, spat in the face of darkness as only play can do. How he and Jane had talked and laughed, the wine bottle between them, their bare toes (hers long and scarlet tipped) touching each other on the porch railing, Silas away giving papers. Jane read him the Rossettis, she read him Leonard Cohen, she read him Richard Brautigan; her gypsy skirts, spangled and bright, swagged down behind her bare knees; her sandals on the floor were silver as fish. In his dream, Jane took Sebastian by the hand and they flew to the bin where Silas had thrown all mementoes of her when she left. In real life Sebastian had crept there after midnight, bereft, desperate, shamed by his need, and found for his dumpster diving one cracked snapshot of his lost love, which he still kept tucked between the pages of Watermelon Sugar. Silas must have burned the rest. Jane the Dream scooped out sheaves of photos, a hundred glossy prints, among them the impossible image he longed for, the never taken snapshot of himself and Jane with their feet on the porch rail. She tucked them into his arms, kissed him, looked back at him and turned to mist. "O Jane!" he cried, "Come back! Don't leave again!"

Across the hall from one another two old men wept into their pillows.

Beth and Orin Stanley were sleeping with the dead. Beth lay in the sagging bed of her uncle's summer camp with her big sister Marjorie, who at fifteen was still three years away from her last fatal car ride. She could hear the waves lick the lakeshore, and Tex Ritter on the radio downstairs. She was completely happy. Orin, not yet "Stan" to anyone, napped by his mother's side on the cot in their big kitchen. Smothered Beef was slow-cooking in the Dutch oven. Orin liked Smothered Beef, and he loved his mother, and he was pretty pleased with first grade too. Sleet rattled the window but the kitchen was warm. Orin was content. In their bed at the Groves, Beth and Orin moved closer together. They dovetailed into one another's empty places.

Glenda Kent had spent the time after supper arranging her clothes in her new closet. Students never did know how to file. Asleep now, she dreamed of closets. Revisiting her first apartment, or perhaps her mother's house, she couldn't tell, she found that she had left in her bedroom closet some clothes that she barely remembered. Were they wearable? Brighter colors, younger styles than she wore now, some of them might no longer be suitable. And could she still get into them? But trying them on she found that she was younger than she'd thought, not out of her thirties by the look of it. Her waist was small enough, her bosom high. All those clothes, hers again! The Depression child in her crowed with joy, but nobody heard her. And in every pocket she found sugar packets and soap. Supplies.

"Thatcher Stewart Sinclair" said the reader of names, and Thatch mounted the stage to kneel in front of the Chancellor, whose academic robe was stiff with gold braid, and then he was Doctor Sinclair. He said to himself that more fuss would be made in Sweden, where they fired cannons, but at any rate he could fly like a shaman, and he stepped off the edge of the stage. And then he was swooping over the heads of the shocked audience, many of them well known anthropologists,

who cried "You've broken the secret!" That's what se-
crets are for, Thatch said to himself, but aloud he an-
swered, If you wanted the golden bough you *should
have kissed Jessie Weston.*

Herbert Christmas, like colleagues past, present,
and future, was dreaming of things left undone, the
ecclesiastical version of the class not met for a whole
semester. It was nearly Advent, and he'd not preached
since Ascension Sunday, nor doled out communion to
penitent and hung-over students, nor kept his counsel-
ing hours to soothe the suicidal. God was going to kill
him.

Harlow and Millie, who slept very little of late,
dozed in and out as they lay side by side with their fin-
gers touching. They were both deeply satisfied to be on
A Wing, and not in fact for the better kitchens. Millie
knew that Harlow had been, in spite of his democratic
principles, shamed at finding himself with the border-
line demented of C Wing, and she had felt it for him.
Harlow knew that Millie understood that and had cov-
ered her joy with talk of baking. Though she would in
fact bake.

For Lily Hillman the border between waking and

sleeping was growing blurred by her own will. She had recognized Sebastian after a fashion, and in fact remembered with pleasure their evenings on the rocks of Schoodic Point, but now her desires were for water, not rock, for the dream and not for the waking. She ate and drank what was given her, dressed herself minimally, and held her consciousness in a fluid state, ready for the submersion of sleep. Deeper and deeper she sank into darkness, though the sensuous sea grass, through the tickling shoals of small fish. She had spent her academic life in the study of the codfish, for no reason that she could any longer remember. Codfish, while she dreamed of Bathypolypus arcticus, the curvaceous deep-sea octopus, or of Architeuthis, the giant squid with his twenty-foot tentacles! Now, her codfish life over, she was free to drift across the bed of the ocean, seeking the touch and curl of things that lurked in caves; she flirted, she floated, while bliss seemed to undulate just ahead. The courtship itself was pleasure. She breathed water like a fish and in the morning found it unremarkable after a night in the sea that her bed was wet and her skin wrinkled.

Chelsea Weighs In

When Chelsea Dean, student intern, arrived at the Groves the following morning, tapping her tongue bolt gently against her lower teeth to soothe her nerves, the first person she saw was Silas. Still in his bathrobe, he was fastening a quotation to his own door, something that he hoped would offset the macabre imagery in Sebastian's odd greeting. It wouldn't do, he thought, for the women to be exposed to Sebastian's taste; it was his solemn duty to protect women. In his anxious hours of wakefulness he had hit on the right passage, from Tennyson's "Ulysses":

> Tho' much is taken, much abides; and tho'
> We are not now that strength which in old days
> Moved earth and heaven; that which we are, we are.

Put that in your dirty pipe and smoke it, Sebastian, Silas thought. He was still strong enough to tidy up his little corner of the world, A Wing at least if not the Groves itself. Brighten the corner where you are.

Chelsea read it. Be nice, be nice to the residents, be nice, she chanted to herself. Oh god, does he really think he ever moved heaven and earth? He was just, like, some sad little professor. "Nice," she said aloud, "that's a nice quote." In fact she found the one on the opposite door more fun, and prettier, but whichever old fart had put that up wasn't here to be nice to, and this one was. This one had pale horrible legs.

Quotation, Silas thought, quotation, dammit, not "quote."

The governing board of the Groves had realized, somewhat belatedly, that the new mix of residents would require the supervision of four wings, not just C and D. Extra nurses were not in the budget, but students with cell phones might do, they reckoned, students who could call nurses as needed and who could plan and oversee social gatherings, which seemed advisable now that the wings would not be coherent in the same way. For instance, the A's and B's now on C and D would need some diversion, and perhaps want to see their former wing mates. Chelsea had been sent from Special Ed, on the premise that one compromised population was a lot like another. She had never meant to take up with the old, the old gave her the horrors, they were real Stephen King in her opinion, but here she was and she was committed to keeping a journal, both to provide details for her own final report and because her boyfriend, an English major, thought that King would soon need a successor and he could be ready. He was counting on her notes for something gross.

"Are you here to visit someone?" Silas asked. "It's very early. Or are you doing a project? I see that you have a notebook." And a tongue bolt, he added mentally. Ye gods, a tongue bolt.

"I'm the student liaison," said Chelsea, "I'm here to, you know, call the nurses and organize activities. I might make some notes." Oh ack, she thought, he's got those horrible old-man cloth slippers on! Who the hell sells those anymore? I have NEVER, make that NEVER seen them in a store. Do these people know how to go online?

"We have some very respectable residents," Silas said with a pursed mouth that suggested otherwise even to Chelsea, who hadn't seen much mouth pursing. "You may want to be a little cautious around Doctor Sinclair, who is having some personal issues and isn't always quite, well, fully dressed." His heart was stirred by the thought that a young woman might once again need his protection. It had been for him a secret and visceral pleasure, the rescue of maidens; the emotional highs of his life had come with waving the sword of his outrage at whichever dastard of a colleague had exposed young females to unwholesome reading or otherwise pained their sensibilities. He, Silas, single handed, had sheltered them from the world, yes, even the ones with spiked hair.

"Yeah, thanks," said Chelsea (be nice, be nice),who felt that whatever bit old Dr. Sinclair was airing couldn't be much more depressing than the white hairless shanks in front of her. She both hoped and feared that it would be what she suspected: a shriveled flasher would be a thing to write about. What did the old have left in that department anyway? Or in any department, she thought as she met the others, who emerged from their doors at various hours; some preferred coffee and high-fiber cereal in their rooms to facing their peers over poached eggs. One man said something cheerful that seemed to be in Klingon, another winked at her, or maybe had something in his eye. "Do you need anything?" she asked the women in wheelchairs, as she had been instructed to do. "Dry sheets," said one of them, and Chelsea cell-phoned the nurses' station. Bedwetting, she reckoned, was not in her job description.

Thatch spent the morning in his room being honest with himself. This was sometimes hard work, though perhaps less hard than when he had been young and hadn't known himself for as long. He had always tried. Now he faced the unlikelihood that anything would come of his so-called study, that he would ever get enough material for an article, that such an article would be of any scholarly value or that anyone would publish it. So why did he go on? Had he simply become, in his retirement, a dirty old man? But no, that was not it exactly. The thrill of showing himself was not the expectation of any sexual outcome, nor did he hope for cries of admiration. Truth be told, he would have preferred cries of outrage. What he wanted, he concluded, was once again to make a stir, as he had formerly done with outré assertions, iconoclastic theories, loose-cannon proposals in faculty meetings. He remembered the stunned faces of his students, the rage of his colleagues. How sweet it had been. Thatcher Sinclair had been a character, a wild man, yet held his job, and for that he had loved the academic life even as he stirred it up. And now he could, perhaps, under the mask of senility, get away with some things that would have undone him in his prime. That was the way to look at it. Flashing made a break in his boredom. The air felt kind on his penis. And for god sake sooner or later someone was going to have to get upset.

Thus the moments before lunch found him strolling along the corridor with renewed purpose, one hand on his zipper pull and another on the notebook that had so far been his excuse. Aware of a presence, he whirled and unzipped.

Harlow and Millie considered him. "Now you just put that away, Thatcher," Millie said, "nobody needs to see it."

"Xrawgr?" said Harlow.

"Yes dear," said Millie. "We have one too, and I think ours is nicer." She hugged his elbow.

The cruelty of virtuous women! Thatch, wilted in every way, turned his back to put himself in order and found that he was facing Chelsea, also with notebook in hand. They both jumped a little, and each, amused at the other's reaction, grinned.

"Dude," Chelsea said kindly, "you'd get more play if you could, like, get it up." She considered that it was the most authentically nice thing she'd said to a resident all day.

Sebastian also, though he had not seen fit to mention it, had been amused by Thatcher's project. He had always enjoyed Thatch, whose more provocative remarks in committee meetings had often kept him, Sebastian, from keeling over from boredom and falling off his chair like a dead parrot off a perch. He had understood, even before Thatch himself did, what was behind the exhibition; it was the consuming desire for incident, and he seconded that motion with all his heart. But if he tried to convey this, and some exciting argument about strategy ensured, he could flip into oratorio again, and he was damned if he was going to find himself babbling about Thatcher's parts, private parts, dick-dock private dick.

He was also aware of the indignation that had provoked Silas's Tennyson riposte, and he reckoned that although he had so far thought of no way to help Thatch along, he could at least keep Silas fanned and burning. The Rossetti lines had been offered in good faith and implicitly reproved. Bite me, Silas, thought Sebastian. Making notes with his books around him, he felt the warlike joy of piling up snowballs behind a fort.

And so, from hour to hour, we ripe and ripe, And then, from hour to hour, we rot and rot:

And thereby hangs a tale.

"Shakespeare trumps Tennyson!" Sebastian thought as he tacked the new passage to the notice board on his door.

From Chelsea's notebook: So gross! If this is really anything like Special Ed I'm changing majors tomorrow. It's like they're aliens, some don't talk at alt some talk so you cant make it out. Oh god getting old must suck. How can they stand each other? How can they stand themselves? The men's leg hair is gone and its sticking out their ears and noses. I've seen grungy old white ankles, a woman who pees her bed and doesn't care, a limp dick flasher, a guy who chokes his food and spits it up, two old profs having a quote fight. There was a film in the lounge and I went to check it out and it was just a bunch of ducks, like a nature film, just ducks and some kind of weeds, no story. Even this bunch deserves more than ducks, no wonder they've gone weird. I'm getting graded on finding them something to do, too. How about Eight Heads in A Dufflebag sometime, I said, that's really fun, but the guy who ran the film had never heard of it. They must all hope every day they'll wake up dead. Me I just hope I'm not the one who finds them if they do.

More Soap

Nobody knew it, how could they, but Glenda Kent had brought with her to A Wing, in two locked suitcases, an impressive collection of soap, in fact soap from all the bathrooms in her old wing into which she had been able to roll while their owners were out. She had done this often, not just in parting, and soon she would need a more capacious hiding place. A minor challenge, she told herself, and not beyond the skill of a good librarian. She did not share Thatcher's devotion to the examined life, and the reasons of her theft had shifted and evolved without her conscious participation. At first, with the onset of mild and not very noticeable dementia, she had become convinced that since the Groves issued soap and other bathroom necessities to its residents, soap ought by rights to be checked out and returned when not in use. Some of the earlier cakes, in fact, bore her crudely incised data—borrower's initials, room numbers, dates of acquisition—in a column that looked not surprisingly like a Dewey Decimal notation. Later she supposed that she was punishing the soap holders, that for some reason connected with the reading of filthy literature they were unworthy of cleaning themselves. Occasionally she supposed that the cakes of soap were gifts to her or gifts that she had purchased for others. But by the time she arrived in A-Wing she had been overtaken by the simple and unreasoning greed of the collector. For Glenda, a cake of soap was ivory, was jasper, was topaz, and bathrooms were the caves of Aladdin.

The first of A-Wing's soap went missing after the weekend, and Orin Stanley was the first person to notice the loss.

"Beth!" he shouted from the shower, "where's the SOAP?"

Orin usually had the shower first, so Beth was still half asleep. Men, she thought. "Try the sink," she called, and rolled over.

She guessed rightly that Orin was shouting from anxiety, though she only half knew why. When he confirmed on a rising note that there was NO SOAP, no soap ANYWHERE, she pulled out of her bedside stand a piece of hotel soap from their anniversary trip to Portland. She liked souvenirs but supposed that the wrapper alone would serve well enough.

Orin had two secret terrors about aging and he kept them to himself, or tried to. Aging further, that is, than he already had. Aging into real old-fart status, losing who he was. The first fear was dirtiness. He'd seen it too often, old men who lost interest in clean socks, began to smell bad, had toilet paper hanging down the inside of a pants leg, and that was while they still bothered with toilet paper and remembered what pants were for. Their old faces were the gray of unwashed skin; their creases, full of darker grime, stood out like roads on a soiled map. He remembered his grandpa, as clean as most until somehow overnight he had gullies of tobacco juice from the corners of his mouth to his unshaven chin, and when he'd asked for his usual kiss and Orin couldn't do it they'd both cried. A bad memory. Stan the Jan, who had cleaned up so many things in his career, was scared blue of the day when he wouldn't care any more, would think he'd only worn those socks three days or he didn't need a shower again tonight he'd had one last Sunday. That, and then filthy old age. It was a slippery slope.

The other thing that got the wind up him was silent pockets. The day his pants went mute would be the day he might as well lie down in his box. If a man's pockets don't have keys and loose change and a jackknife, Orin believed, then he isn't a man. Calling on Beth's dad in a nursing home one day, he'd noticed when a visitor walked by that the guy jingled—he was slamming his fists around in his pockets, not too happy to visit maybe, and then Orin realized that the men who lived there were silent at least silent in the pockets. There were noises of shuffling and farting and sometimes shouting, but no clink of metal.

Ever since he'd figured that out, those pockets were his vision of real life over with, the after-time when he'd lost his power over locks, when there was nothing to buy and no knots to cut. He'd made Beth promise him he could have keys when he went gaga even if they didn't fit anything. She'd laughed. "You want to die like a janitor, do you?" Like a man, he thought, but he couldn't say it.

"Harlow, are you hiding my soap?" Millie called with the playfulness he loved, and he laughed till he had a choking fit. It was their old way of joking, each accusing the other of absurd escapades, but they hadn't done it for a while because Harlow's part was a little hard to pull off. All the same, the soap was gone. They looked in all the likely places and then in some unlikely ones to make each other laugh. At least, Millie said, they still had toothpaste.

At supper the two A-Wing couples had begun to share a table. Beth liked to be with Millie, and as far as he could tell, Millie enjoyed Beth, she was a damned fool if she didn't. Harlow's choking and spewing didn't bother him; he'd unplugged toilets, for god sake, and before he had enough seniority to avoid it he'd cleaned up after student parties. Harlow was nothing. The guy seemed happy and it was a hoot to see what Millie would claim he'd said.

"It's the funniest thing," Millie said over the froth of her ice pudding, "but our bathroom soap just disappeared today. We had to wash up in plain water, didn't we, Harlow?" Harlow croaked agreement.

"So did ours!" said Beth. "They'll give us some more from housekeeping, but where did it go? You don't suppose that tongue-bolt girl took it?"

"No," said Orin. "Students steal one cake of soap or one lawn chair, or whatever they think they need at the moment. Hell, they'd steal one of us if they thought we were still good for anything. Or on a bet some guy steals all the chalk on campus. But two cakes of soap?— doesn't sound like student work."

Orin was right, Harlow thought. Janitors often, in his experience, saw through the workings of academic behavior at all levels and they could tell it straight. He did not envy Orin's way with words. He was finding his own incapacity profoundly restful. He had spoken too much in his life; his job seemed one endless oration, his voice flowing like syrup over meetings, down from lecterns, oozing into the ears of secretaries and prospective students. He had come to dislike the smooth sound of it and had sometimes gone on automatic pilot and ceased to listen. Now Millie was Aaron to his Moses, she spoke in his place, and if she did not always get it right she got it right often enough, since nothing he said mattered anyway. He quite liked the harsh gravel of his post stroke croak, but what was the point of it? He nodded, though, and gave Stan a double thumbs up.

"Gosh-all-fishhooks," thought Stan, "he's still in there. How in hell does the poor bugger keep smiling?"

Three days later, Beth and Millie were sharing a pot of tea and a plate of lemon bars while Harlow napped.

For both of them it seemed a return to life before Gold-engroves, when they had sat down to chat with real women, whereas many of the women at the Groves seemed, if not exactly imaginary, at least two dimensional. Or if real, then not normal, thought Beth. For her there was an extra pleasure in the afternoon, remembering how she and Millie had moved in different circles, Millie at the top of the college, she in town. Harlow Osgood's wife could have been a snob, but that was the last thing anyone would say of Millie. For Millie, as a matter of fact, Beth felt like home and family, like the neighbors of her girlhood; she had not, after all, been born in a college infirmary or raised in a lab, she had been Millie Hanson of Greenville, Maine, and her dad had run a hunting lodge.

"Okay," said Beth, picking up the conversation, "you and I didn't take the soap, and our husbands didn't take the soap or we'd know it."

Millie nodded. "Sebastian Antioch is secretive," she said, "but whatever he's hiding probably isn't soap. He's got his head in books."

"Yes," said Beth, "and he put out a note for housekeeping that said 'More Soap Please,' so he's probably lost his too."

"Unless he's eating it," Millie joked, "and wanting seconds."

"Silas is the one who'd eat it," Beth said. "Lord almighty, that man is taken up with purity. Orin says he can't —excuse me—pass wind without Silas popping up with a gas meter."

"Oh, I wish it would be Silas!" they admitted in unison and, laughing, spluttering into their hands so as not to wake Harlow, they remembered how it had felt to make a new best friend.

THE CHIVALRY QUESTION

Barely a week later, Silas took the literary offensive and in the small hours pinned to his door, with all the triumph of Martin Luther at Wittenberg, a favorite passage from Charles Kingsley. When Sebastian, finding himself out of coffee, emerged for breakfast, a sheet of paper in Silas's tidy handwriting caught his eye:

Some say the age of chivalry is past, that the spirit of romance is dead. The age of chivalry is never past, so long as there is a wrong left unredressed on earth.

Bugger, thought Sebastian, that's a strong lead. Romantic AND capital-v virtuous.

As a prelude to subversion, he put a good deal more butter and jam on his toast than was advisable for anyone over seventeen and enjoyed it while he thought. His job was to present the opposing view and thereby to irritate Silas, who in his heart objected to the existence, let alone the expression, of contradictory opinions. So what was he to assert? That the age of chivalry was past beyond all sighting, that the age of chivalry had never been chivalrous, that the illusion of modern knighthood was the last refuge of jackasses? He would have liked to write the rebuttal himself, but that was not the game. The romantic vision, he mused—what trumps it? It would hold up against crabbiness, gloom, nay-saying, and expletives. He had listed and crossed these out on his paper napkins, which he now used to wipe butter off his mustache.

"Sebastian," said Herbert Christmas in passing. "Ah," said Sebastian.

Cynicism, he thought, cynicism and wit. There's very little that can stand against humor, thank god.

Thinking of God, who had made wit and metaphor, the God of Donne, he looked with some fondness at the unassuming back of Herbert Christmas, Divinity's representative at the Groves. Perhaps he should at least have said,

"Ah, Herbert." Christmas wasn't a bad sort, after all, despite his unfortunate name, and had done his job as chaplain with diligence and decency, as far as Sebastian could tell. The thought of Herbert actually called up the word "Christian"—a compliment to his performance and not an inevitable connection, Sebastian reckoned—and that word led him to his answer:

Byron was just the ticket. The response would be a little oblique, to be sure, but it had the advantage of being poached from the 19th century, ordinarily Silas's favorite preserve. Not that anyone owned territory, exactly, as chairman after exasperated chairman had pointed out when devising course assignments. They had all been hired as generalists at a time when the college was still small, they were expected to teach anywhere in British or American literature that they were needed, but all the same their aesthetic and philosophical predilections sharpened and became known. Sebastian loved the 17th century best, Silas the 19th, while other colleagues might be drawn to the centuries of Gower or Congreve or Auden.

Back in his apartment, Sebastian washed his hands and printed in large letters:

A QUIET CONSCIENCE MAKES ONE SO SERENE! CHRISTIANS HAVE BURNT EACH OTHER, QUITE PERSUADED THAT ALL THE APOSTLES WOULD HAVE DONE AS THEY DID.

Yes, chivalry damned well is dead, Silas, he thought, *if it ever existed. For which there doesn't seem to be a whole lot of evidence in human nature as I've known it, and that would include yours.*

No-Kegger

Homemade posters of limited artistic merit appeared in the lounges and at the turnings of the corridors, letting the residents know that Chelsea and her peers in the geriatric internship were having a shot at a decent grade. The simple text had involved some discussion.

"All-Wings Get-Together?" Morgan had suggested, crayon poised, but "Won't they think that's about the food?" Kelly asked. Discussion followed: Had these old people ever eaten Buffalo wings? Had there always been Buffalo wings? How important were teeth, could they gum the flesh off the little bones?

Ashleann brought them back to the point. "Like, we're having cookies?

And little squishy sandwiches? Not Buffalo wings? So let's just make the posters?" The other girls understood that none of these were questions.

WINGS A-B-C-D

P-A-R-T-Y

FOOD—GAMES—MUSIC SORRY, NO BEER

WEDNESDAY AFTERNOON 3-5

They drew pictures of balloons in the corners, not that balloons were part of the original plan but they were easy to draw and should be recognizable even by the very far gone.

"Not much of a party without a keg," said Kelly.

"Godsake," said Chelsea, "they're gross enough sober. You want to clean up puke, you can."

Even the residents who disliked parties, who had indeed disliked them from childhood, who bore psychic scars from Musical Chairs and Sadie Hawkins dances, felt a small lift of the spirits at the sight of the posters. It was, perhaps, the notion that someone wished them well, or the even more illusory idea that the young would care to socialize with them. Within half an hour the more astute remembered that they had fallen for such lures before and that disillusionment had followed as the night the day. Still, most of them intended to risk it again.

Silas was remembering a department chair who had brought brownies to their meetings and thereby made grandstanding sweeter yet; he felt as though he had tasted neither brownies nor power for a long time.

Brownies, at least, might still be possible. Sebastian reckoned that with some vigilance he could still manage lighthearted chatter. At a party he could stop his mouth with a sandwich and walk away if his linguistic needle showed signs of getting stuck. Of the others on A Wing, the best pleased were Millie, who had always rather liked parties, and Orin, who expected little from the Food-Games-Music but a fair lot of fun from watching the senile at their sports.

It looked as though none of them would be disappointed. The girls, inspired by their own drawings, had shaken down their friends for leftover decorations. The results, if oddly mixed—pink streamers, a paper palm tree, an inflatable Budweiser NASCAR, and a number of balloons advocating safe sex—were festive and no stranger a mix than the party goers themselves, with their wheelchairs, walkers, and limps, their various calls and cries, from which Sebastian was able to distinguish "God have mercy!" "Arsenic in it!" and "Call the question!" as well as less articulate cries that would rivet an ornithologist. He was interested to see that Lily was fully dressed, even to a string of beads, and appeared to be fully present in her body. Ordinarily, he had noticed, she occupied it until noon or thereabouts but began to drift away after lunch. Lily had made some effort.

Silas was happy to see that brownies were, after a fashion, on the menu; they were not those dense treats he remembered, with a little cracked glaze on top, they were smaller and tidier, but chocolate nonetheless. Small brownies, small powers, he thought. The sandwiches were, as Ashleann had foretold, small and squashy, but convenient, Herbert Christmas told himself as he crept up on the cookies, for his brothers and sisters with no teeth. He wondered whether the treats would be better if the residents with kitchens, like Millie, could be given ingredients and turned loose. There was a general if halting rush for the bowls of potato chips that Kelly had insisted on. Old people, as it h1rned out, liked salt and didn't get enough of it. Morgan, watching, thought of the salt licks on her uncle's farm.

Sebastian and Lily, face to face over the chip bowls, remembered the crash of waves.

"Rogue," said Lily, amused. Wild Lily Hillman, the hot new hire, looked out at him for a moment.

"Wench," Sebastian countered, and felt like himself.

"That was a fine time," he added, and he meant all of it, the sense of starting out, the risk of getting caught, the fine instruments of their bodies, the salt air. She was no Jane Bassett, but they'd rung some bells.

"Braggart," said Lily, and rolled away laughing. But we were only on the rocks, not in the water, she thought, and that was no twenty-foot tentacle.

There was more of Lily Hillman left than he'd supposed, Sebastian mused. Perhaps she could be persuaded to shriek a little one day for Thatcher's morale.

"Now if you've all had refreshments," Morgan said in rehearsed phrases, as she sat down on the piano bench, "how about some singing?"

The girls had been sure that a piano was good but had been uncertain about the content of a sing-along. Had they better understood the social ineptitude of many who would later become professors or librarians, they might have given up on it, but Special Ed children responded well to group singing, or as well as could be expected, and in that field the girls had all had been trained.

They had ransacked their memories for songs old and corny enough to suit this gang. "Old MacDonald

Had a Farm"? "She'll be Coming Round the Mountain"?

"All together," cried Morgan, "on 'The Teddy Bears' Picnic!'"

A ripple of alarm crossed the room. "Move we adjourn!" shrilled someone's voice, and "No quorum!" chattered several others. The lucid squirmed with humiliation: how the hell senile did these girls think they were?

"It's not real bears," Kelly said, in case that was what ailed them. "It's only teddy bears."

"We'll sing it for you? And then you can pick next?" Ashleann suggested, and the four girls, with more diligence than zest, sang of disguised expeditions to the woods. 'In disguise' indeed, thought Sebastian. These girls have no idea what it's like not to recognize your own face. He thought of commedia dell' arte with its mask of the old man. Pantalone, gullible and amorous. Things to watch out for.

"Okay, so one of you pick," Chelsea said when they finished.

"Ninety-nine Bottles of Beer on the Wall," said Thatcher, and aged voices took it up at once with something like relief. At least it would last a good long time.

He could hear Orin's tenor lead the tune until Morgan pulled herself together. Herbert Christmas, relieved as anyone, was singing it with the false gusto peculiar to clergy on an outing. Random numbers rose into the musical slipstream from those who had long ago lost count, or other things, but sang on —three, thirty, five-teen, three, forty-seven, twelve, three, eleventy-nine, undid, arsenic.

As the fifty-ninth bottle fell from the walt Glenda quietly wheeled herself from the room, visions of un-guarded bathrooms dancing in her head. Millie and Beth, sitting only three tables from the door, poked each other and mouthed Aha. Weighing Glenda and Lily as possible soap thieves, they had put their money on Glenda.

"It's the larcenous librarian," Millie said just below the music. "Did you hide your soap?" asked Beth.

"It's in Harlow's spare shoes," Millie said. "She can't look there, it's too low down, she'd fall on her face!"

Too late they saw Silas within earshot, the maidens' champion waking in his eyes. Oh shit oh dear, thought Millie. Crappity damn, thought Beth, he's got us.

"I hope," said Silas at his stiffest "that you're not

even considering accusing that fine woman, handicapped as she is, of being anything less than a lady. I won't stand for that." And he marched away before they could imagine what to say or where to hit him.

*

From Chelsea's notebook: Never never never try to do crafts with old people, especially with paint and probably glue or glitter too. Being this is November we thought they'd like to make some of those handprint-turkey things like we used to make in first grade. Easy, right? Turns out most of them couldn't put their hands down flat to make a turkey, who knew, and half of them spilled the paint trying, and some of the ones who spilled cried and oh it sucked sucked sucked. Red paint all over the tables and the floor and the people. It looked like after some major battle in the Civil War or something, except that none of them were actually laying on the floor. Then we tried to clean their hands up and the nurse had to open the supply closet because nobody could find any soap. What the hell was that about? Do they eat it? Hide it up their butts? And why was old Silas so extra pissed about it? We'll get a C- on that party if we're lucky, Morgan says.

Kelly says a D+. Ashleann was crying too hard to guess, she really needs the grade. Me, I think we're screwed.

RUDE ARMOR

The more Silas thought about the slur on Glenda Fessette's integrity, the more indignant he became. This was not unpleasant: indignation warmed and energized him. Therefore he encouraged it, adding small increments of insult as one feeds twigs to a growing flame. He could not have said why he wished to defend Glenda against defamation rather than Millie and Beth against theft; when the woman appeared whose champion he must be, he knew her, that was all. The old librarian's single state, her evident lack of a protector, was less a factor, perhaps, than an excuse. True, he preferred his maidens younger, but in a context where helplessness mattered more than heaving bosoms, he could make do. He squared his shoulders and thought of how catty Beth had looked as she joked with Millie at the party. As for when and where to confront them, the chance would come: he was doing the work of righteousness.

On the following Thursday, Glenda stayed in her room during dinner, saying that she felt unwell. This show of fragility wrenched Silas's inflamed heart. She was, he feared, suffering the pangs of calumny, alone and weeping. He longed to go to her and could not. Even now, at the table occupied by the couples, the two women, looking to Silas offensively robust, chatted and laughed, leaning in for confidentiality. He assumed that they were making fun of Glenda (and in that he was, as a matter of fact, correct). He saw that their men did not chastise them, but seemed amused. The one sex was as reprehensible as the other.

The couples saw Silas rise and head for their table, judgment in his eyes. "Oh crap," said Beth, "here he comes."

Orin sat up straight. He was by and large a peaceful man, but he did not propose that his wife be called to account by some dickless twerp with a comb-over, not while he had a fist left to clench. He saw that Harlow was tensing too, and wondered for the first time whether the old boy had any punch left in him. "Orin," Beth whispered, "—heart." This was not a call to compassion, Orin knew, but a medical reminder in case he was tempted to throw Silas out a window.

"Silas," Millie was saying in a voice smooth as custard, "what can we do for you?"

Slick, thought Harlow, and rested a hand on the small of her back. "I have come to speak to you girls," Silas announced.

Beth failed to suppress a giggle. How many times had she heard her old headmaster say those words with just such sternness? Was Silas planning to put her on restriction?

"There are no girls here, Silas," Millie said, and the custard was gone. "Beth and I are women. I in fact am an old woman."

"Then why don't you act like one!" Silas cried, but that was a mistake. "O Harlow," Millie quavered, "where are my specs? I can't see to do my tatting!" The other three whooped.

The conversation was not going at all well, Silas thought. They were like some unruly class, not quite over high school, who talked in the back row and cared not a whit for his disquisition on William Bradford. He did not suspect that they hoped to forestall the moment when Orin might have to deck him.

"I am HERE to SPEAK to you," he said, and pulled up an uninvited chair. " ... thou fearful guest," murmured Beth, in whom Silas with his accidental imitation of her headmaster had set off explosions of high-school memory like a string of tiny firecrackers.

"Who with thy hollow breast/ Still in rude armor drest,/ Comest to daunt me!" Millie added. She belonged to a generation that had memorized. In the days when they could both speak, she and Harlow had been famous among their friends for their two-part rendition of "The Cremation of Sam McGee."

So they know Longfellow, Silas thought. Well it won't save them from the wrath to come.

"You were, and are, most disrespectful to Miss Fessette," Silas scolded on a rising note, "and I won't have it!"

"What," said Millie, unimpressed, "because we hide our soap? None of his business, is it, Harlow?"

"Mafft," growled Harlow, and for once there was no mistaking his meaning.

"Won't have it?" said Orin, leaning back. "I'll tell you what you will have, Doctor Bassethound, you'll have Orin Stanley on your back if you ever dare tell my wife what to say, and speaking for Harlow, the same goes for Millie!" His hand yearned towards a grip on Silas's tie. His fingers twitched.

"Silas," Millie broke in, smiling. "We are university people, though out to pasture, and it is our right to seek truth without hindrance, is it not? Now to the four of us, and I might add to a number of other people, Glenda appears to be stealing soap. She appears to be, perhaps by reason of dementia, a thief.

That is our truth."

"But it's NOT true!" Silas cried. "She's innocent as a lamb! You are causing her pain, you're making her ill, I know it! You have to stop! Suppose I accused Beth of stealing slippers, how would you feel then?"

Harlow and Millie fixed him with the look of pitying disdain familiar to veterans of college meetings, the look that never fails at once to squelch and to madden. Beth and Orin did their best to copy it. Their expressions were close enough to be recognizable.

"There are such things as anti-defamation laws!" Silas cried, wheeling to stalk away. "You haven't heard the last of this!"

"No doubt," Millie and Beth said together, and laughed till they feared for their underwear.

As for Orin, his damaged heart was singing: he'd finally dissed a professor and there was not one thing left in the world that anybody could fire him from.

Songs of Thankfulness and Praise

By tradition, Thanksgiving dinner at Goldengroves took place on the Monday before college break. In theory this permitted residents of the Groves to spend the holiday with their families, though in fact very few of them did. Some of them would have struck terror to the heart of any family gathering, some had never married and had no siblings left, many had children who had scattered to other states. The real reason, as they well knew and to which they did not object was that the shldent chefs planned to go home; if dinner was going to be lavish it was going to be early as well. On Thanksgiving itself the college food service would give them hot turkey sandwiches, which they also liked, for they missed holiday leftovers. In previous years each wing had eaten in its own cozy dining room, but in this year of mainstreaming, two wings would dine together at parallel tables in one of the lounges. The linen cloths, the centerpieces, reminded those who had once lived in a dorm of the thrill it had been to go to dinner in what they called a real house. The dessert table, too, caught many an eye: sh1dent chefs vied in the production of Thanksgiving pies for the Groves—cherry walnut, peach crumb, brandied squash, chocolate coconut, creme de menthe, as well as nostalgic favorites like lemon meringue and graham cracker and apple. Pie Heaven, thought Herbert Christmas.

After A Wing had sat down, after D Wing, its partner du jour, had variously sat or been rolled in or strapped down, after Herbert had said grace and plates of artfully arranged food had been set before them, Millie rapped on her glass. "Harlow and I," she said, "are a little old-fashioned"—pause for laughter—"and we always like to observe with our friends the custom of saying what makes us thankful."

Orin was not the only one to think *Yeah? How's that working out for Harlow?*

"Speaking for both of us," Millie went on, "we're thankful for our friends and family and most of all for each other; we've never stopped being sweethearts." Harlow rasped and nodded. *Obviously she has to speak for both of us,* he thought *and it's true enough, I still love her, but what I'm really thankful for is that I have never since my stroke had to play Millie's Thanksgiv-*

ing game, and unless some treacherous miracle occurs, I will never have to play it again. He patted her hand with affection.

Glenda and Lily were used to the custom from C Wing and had often risen to Millie's lead with gratitude for peace and clement weather, high-toned but blood-less observations that made honest gratitude for pie too homely to utter. On A Wing, a year deeper into demen-tia, Glenda had just enough command of her wits to censor allusions to soap. "I'm...Glenda," she said," and I'm thankful for....the Dewey Decimal system!" She blushed with pleasure at the laughter. There's a woman who appreciates order, Silas thought.

Thank God, Lily thought, I can drop the sunshine bit. "And I" she said, "am thankful to be through with codfish."

"Turkey!" came a cry from D Table, where someone had lost the idea of scholarship and believed her to be talking about dinner.

A tense silence fell. Millie understood the discom-fort of the diners and she was sorry for it, at least a little. But if you couldn't hang onto your rituals, what was there? Of course the exercise of thankfulness might be good for them, no doubt it would, but mostly it would be good for her. I've been nice to all of them, she thought, and they are just going to have to do this for me. She knew enough of pedagogy to understand that if she out-waited them they'd break, and she had the patience to do it. She caught Beth's eye.

Knowing she owed it, Beth stood up. "I am thankful for a new friend," she said. And that was true, but secretly she was also thankful not to be married to any of the other men there, including Thatcher and Sebastian, though those two she considered somewhat hot in an aged kind of way.

Good for Beth, Orin thought, but it didn't mean he was going to play. He was thankful for plenty of things, but he didn't see that they were anybody's goddamn business. His defensiveness, had he known it, mirrored that of the more lucid professors, who feared to reveal an undefended chink in their psychic armor. They well remembered the vicious volatility of academia, they had seen colleagues pulled down like a caribou in a wolf pack not only for errors but for the format of their erratum sheets. The silence vibrated with calculation. Orin counted his treasures for the sheer secrecy of it:

the fun of watching these assholes carry on; the soft curve of Beth's belly; six kinds of pie; not being really old yet. He sat back and grinned.

Herbert Christmas, too, was thinking PIE, PIE, PIE, and little else, but he was searching for an oblique way, at least, to say it. He knew that duty compelled him to speak soon. "I am thankful," he said at last, "as I am every year, for the bounty of the good Lord."

Pie, agreed a mental chorus around the room. They too were expert, or had been, in language as camouflage.

Thatcher was deeply grateful that Lily had shrieked that morning when he flashed her. He suspected charity and he didn't mind. Charity begets charity, and so he loved her a little. He thought that next time he would anoint himself with butter, attractively shiny if perhaps hard on the shorts. He was not, of course, about to share his thoughts. But Thatcher was, if anything, a good sport who had taken part in many an odd and off-putting ritual in his field work. And now he knew what to say, but not yet how to put it. "I am thankful," he said in the slow considering way that his profession employed to cover a mental void and at the same time make students think that something worth writing down was imminent, "I am thankful for the richness and diversity of human custom, of which our celebration today is but the smallest fraction." How's that for pompous bullshit? he said to himself. I guess this old anthropologist can still sling it.

Sebastian savored a forkful of twice-baked sweet potato and appeared not to notice the gratitude fest, but he was biding his time. He was grateful for a hundred things, past and present, at least three quarters of which could safely be mentioned in mixed company: synonyms, sky rockets, the complete works of Sir Thomas Browne, green tomatoes, Penguin editions, freshly sharpened pencils, for instance; moments of historic defiance, the light on the fir tree outside his window, strong coffee, string quartets. His aim was to let Silas go first, to commit himself to some sentiment that could then be compromised or negated by Sebastian's own cause of gratitude. In this context, unlike the duel of quotations, Silas would not get a turn for rebuttal. In that arena too, however, he had begun to see that he might coax out his antagonist's best shot and then top it. Here's one for Jane, he told himself when he needed a reason, but the fun of zinging his old colleague's complacency was sufficient motive on most days. And I am thankful for the chance, he said to himself.

Silas half guessed Sebastian's plan and wholly abhorred it. No fool himself he calculated at once how long he could delay his own endorsement of right values and saw that it was not enough. He who strolled the corridors and sometimes reproved the erring would be expected to contribute, indeed to have contributed already, while Sebastian, half a hermit, could sit in the shadows and wait like a cat. Silas put down his fork. Going for cosmic was his only chance. "I am thankful," he said, "that the world is an ordered and serious place, that the seasons keep their rounds and the planets their courses." There. That should cost Sebastian something.

Sebastian, on the whole, was pleased. Good one, Silas, he thought. Having expected no less, he had been making a list of possible responses since the ritual began. He ate a bite of chestnut dressing. No need to look over-ready, crucial to stay calm. "I am thankful for surprise," he said at last in the voice that in the old days had skewered many a lame argument in faculty meetings, "surprise, without which order is mere uniformity. Thankful for wild weather and new ideas, wild, yes, whether they suit us or not; for unexpected visitors, funny accidents, mysteries. Joy, that always surprises. Joy, I am thankful for it." And most of al(he thought as he sat back down, I am thankful that I didn't speak oratorio worse than I could cover. At least I don't think I did. There may be a technique to this.

Thank you, thank you, thank you. Turkey had never tasted better.

Millie had lived in Maine for most of her life and knew enough not to push Orin; she recognized his state of mind, which could have been shared by any one of her male relatives. The problem was what to do about the other table.

The hostess in her, the mother in her, and the Vice-Presidential spouse in her, all told her that those others must not be left out. Risky, though, to start them up, for the new transplants looked despondent past all thankfulness, and several long-term residents of D were spatting their gravy with the backs of their spoons or tucking chestnut stuffing about their persons for later. Still, she had to try. "Would any of our friends at D table like to tell us what they're thankful for?" she said.

A woman in a wheelchair, once a nurse in the infirmary, spoke up: "I have a bag of apples!"

"How nice," said Millie. "In your room?"

"No, I have it right here," said the former nurse, who clearly didn't. "Give me one?" said the man who sat across from her.

"Come and get it," she said.

"I'm tied in," he said. "Roll it to me."

"Oh all right," she said, and the idea of apple trundled across the linen.

Orin loved it.

"Anyone else?" said Millie.

"THANKFUL?" shouted the woman who had once terrorized A-Wing with her wheelchair. "What should I be thankful for, shut in this hell hole? When I came to this horrible country I was young and beautiful. You're all against me, you've never been my friends, you don't make me a full professor! You leave my parties early, at others you stay till 2 a.m. and sing. Mine was the best dissertation in my university. My examiners gave me a certificate WRITTEN IN GOLD! Why am I put on this D Wing with all these fools? I am always an A student!"

Such small morale as the D-Wing table might have

possessed fled at her shouts. The transferred professor of art history appeared to be weeping into his plate. He had not escaped her after all. There's mainstreaming for you, thought Silas.

"Shut up, Leonie!" said a one-legged botanist who'd been traded from B- Wing. "I knew you when you were young. You were never all that beautiful."

From nervous tension the other diners at the table began to emit odd ejaculations, cries or phrases that might or might not be related to gratitude— "Banana!" "Goodness and mercy!" "Do it now!" "Kittypants!"

"Well," said an old Accounting prof who had also come from B, "at least we aren't dead yet."

Maybe, thought Thatcher. What's your definition?

Dead people don't have pie, thought Herbert Christmas.

The Foeman's Steel

Sebastian could find no fault with his Thanksgiving-Day insight. He did not care to go on dueling Silas with quotations forever, for he was pained on behalf of the literature. While he was not averse to the idea of whacking Silas with any number of things—rotten cucumbers, say; wet laundry, lawsuits, the back of his hand—he had begun to feel that the passages he loved should not be employed for so low a purpose as goading his colleague. The thing now was to imagine what sentiment Silas admired most and how to lure it out for refutation.

Sebastian lay on his bed flexing his fingers and tried to think himself into Silas's head. I am Silas. I am angry because my wife left me. But no, that was not right. Silas had seemed relieved when Jane left them. It was Sebastian himself who had raged at her loss. I am Silas. I despise the madman across the hall. He has no taste in literature. Closer, but Silas didn't care about taste per se, he cared about content, though he might have used the phrase "good taste" to describe propriety.

I am Silas. I despise frivolity. I despise excess. I despise unwholesomeness.

Unsoundness. Deliberate blindness to the truths I see so clearly. Yes, that was about right. In which case, he could guess what Silas's ultimate quotation might be, and all he would need was a key word to draw it out of him. He could solve that in a flash with a reference book, but he preferred to move slowly and savor the hunt.

Through the window at his bed's foot he saw passages of blue between the scudding clouds. Some fresh air before lunch would be nice. He added to his outdoor clothes a beret and a walking stick, both of which he knew to be reliable irritants. Silas was more of an earflap guy. Also, the walking stick had a flask under the knob, and if he ran into Silas perhaps he'd take a sip, or pretend to. He did not approve of booze in the morning any more than Silas did, in fact, but Silas, who imagined the worst of him, wouldn't know that. The sheer fact of the flask, the way it undercut the seriousness of something close to a cane, would madden him.

On the way out he met Chelsea, back from her long weekend. She looked at him and laughed, but with a note of pleasure. "Hiking?" she suggested, as an absurdity.

"Thinking on the hoof," Sebastian said. "Thinking."

Having failed to meet Silas, Sebastian took off the beret long enough to let the wind blow through his hair. He still had a good head of it, thick and silver.

Well, silver-white. Okay, really white, like his moustache. He would have admired his looks in someone else, he reckoned, someone in whose dark-headed youth he had no personal investment. He faced south towards the unseen ocean that made itself felt in the flavor of the breeze. No, more than a breeze, but less than a gale, a squall, or a tempest. A good blow. Gusty. Boisterous. Lovely words, though he had never cared for the namby-pamby "zephyr." But of course he knew what passage to use on Silas. He had known all along.

"The minstrel boy to the war has gone," he sang to the gulls in a resonant baritone as he turned back, "in the ranks of death you will find him." He gave his walking stick a drum major's flourish. He should sing more; he liked the way the words came out, single file, straight and obedient. He had heard of people who ceased to stutter when they sang, but should he sing his conversation at the Groves, how quickly his fellow patients would declare him senile. Poor Sebastian, they'd say, I fear his mind is going, and deeper down a voice would add, and mine has not. I have outlasted another one. I am still in the land of the normal.

After lunch he pinned up his new quotation, written without emphasis or flourish lest it look like the bait it was. He thought that most people would find it plausibly his, a little melancholy, a little grim, and once again Shakespearean.

Had there been in the Groves someone who knew both Sebastian's special period and Sebastian himself, that person might have found Prospero's famous speech from The Tempest suspiciously obvious. But there was no such person.

We are such stuff

As dreams are made on, and our little life Is rounded with a sleep.

And now, Silas, Sebastian thought as he pressed in the last tack, our revels are at least well on the way to being ended.

For the next day and a half Sebastian watched the blank front of Silas's door as their generation of lovelorn teenagers had once watched for the postman. He did not assume that Silas was rising above the bait; he assumed that Silas was calculating his response, and perhaps teasing him a little as well. Go on, Silas, he thought, play your king, I've got a head full of aces.

When, at last, through the crack of his own door, he spied a sheet of paper on Silas's, his heart came close to a flutter. Clearly he had nowhere near enough to do, he thought, but all the same, when he was close enough to read the first line, "Tell me NOT in mournful numbers," emphasis Silas's, he would have done a little goal-post dance if he'd trusted his balance.

Tell me NOT in mournful numbers,
Life is but an empty dream!
For the soul is dead that slumbers,
And things are not what they seem.
LIFE IS REAL! LIFE IS EARNEST!
And the grave is not its goal;
Dust thou art, to dust returnest,
Was not written of the soul.

"Why, Silas," Sebastian murmured, "those numbers weren't mournful at all! But I 'll be glad to show you mournful if you want it." As he'd foreseen, Silas had been unable to resist the provocation of "dream" and had taken his best shot.

He couldn't get more positive than *A Psalm of Life* without sinking to depths so maudlin that no English professor including Silas would venture there.

Longfellow was legitimate, but some cavillers would say "just." And so Sebastian had him, almost no matter which grim counterweight he chose. Housman? Webster? Larkin? The intellectual cupboard was full to overflowing. And wait, wasn't Silas promoting two points really, the first that life was earnest (a clear slap at Sebastian's perceived frivolity, and Jane's too), the second that death was of secondary importance? If so, Sebastian might shoot back his final volley from both barrels, what fun.

Chesterton would be the man to defend the legitimacy of the light touch: Some think that funny is the opposite of serious. Funny is the opposite of not funny, and of nothing else....whether a man chooses to tell a truth in long sentences of short jokes is a problem analogous to whether he chooses to tell the truth in French or German.

In the end he decided to let his great favorite, Sir

Thomas Browne, supply the coup de grace, not because he was most fit for the job but as one gives an honor to a friend. Honorary pallbearer, for instance, Sebastian thought, grinning. And wasn't it odd, he further thought, taking down *Religio Medici* gently, for its binding was old, that the cranky little pill Silas was such an advocate for the positive side of literature, while he, Sebastian, who ordinarily thought of himself as quite a happy fellow, found more truth in darkness.

Certainly, there is no happiness within this circle of flesh, nor is it in the optics of these eyes to behold felicity: the first day of our jubilee is death. The Devil hath therefore failed of his desires; we are happier with death than we should have been without it.

"Finis," he wrote at the end. Contest over. Checkmate. Death might not be the "goal" of life, he'd never suggested that it was, but it was pretty damn silly at their ages not to get comfortable with the idea.

GOOD LORD DELIVER US

Herbert Christmas had not been able to forget the despair of the Art History professor, Bob, Dave, no, Don, who'd lost all cause for thankfulness, who not even by his sad relocation to D Wing had escaped his wheelchair nemesis.

Freedom from Leonie might have made the general level of chaos on D tolerable, might have made anything short of an afternoon in the Black Hole of Calcutta tolerable, but D Wing and Leonie both! The man was suffering, Herbert admitted, and to such a degree that he had a right to expect compassion from any viable Christian, and more especially from any professional one. He would wander over to D and see how poor Donald was getting on. On A Wing, as in his old department, Don had aroused neither great affection nor yet dislike. An encounter with him had sent no one away brightened, but on A he had enjoyed a kind of unexamined gratih1de for attracting so much of Leonie's venom away from the rest of them. Most of D Wing, Herbert feared, would be past noticing, so the poor fellow would be deprived of even that small warmth. I should have made myself go over sooner, he thought.

The four wings, accessible to one another and yet separate communities, were connected by covered walkways. Herbert could have gone the short way, A to D, but he chose instead to pass through B and C to buy himself time. He drove on his reluctant steps with snatches from Cranmer's Great Litany, an ever-present help in time of trouble. *That it may please thee to inspire us, in our several callings, to do the work which thou givest us to do with singleness of heart as thy servants, and for the common good, we beseech thee to hear us, good Lord.* Perhaps he'd get a glimpse of other still rational colleagues whom he could greet. Perhaps on C Wing he'd call in briefly on Horner and Alphonse, the ancient entomologists, unless they were napping. The older one got, the more one napped, and the closer to death one got, the greater the incentive. Then too, he had set off after lunch--a well seasoned tuna salad on a croissant, with just a hint of fresh celery—when he himself felt most invigorated, but others found the noon meal soporific. He brushed some overlooked pastry flakes from his sweater.

B's corridor, he noted, was carpeted in the same design as A's, dark red with a Greek-key border, though already it looked a little less fresh than A's.

How would the carpet and the mainstreaming get on together, Herbert wondered. He said hello to the music professor who had helped the year Herbert had arranged a program of Christmas music—yes, there'd been jokes— in the college chapel. Anglican classics, "Lo, How A Rose," "Once in Royal David's," lovely, high, spooky stuff. Why had they never done it again? Seasonal revels and exam week were always a poor fit. Lost opportunities.

C Wing's hall was carpeted too, less attractively, in what was clearly an indoor/outdoor product. Incontinence had not been the problem on C, but spilling. *That it may please thee to visit the lonely; to strengthen all who suffer in mind, body, and spirit; and to comfort with thy presence those who are Jailing and infirm, we beseech thee to hear us, good Lord.* Now of course the accidents would be more varied, but Herbert reckoned the carpet would last for a while. He was amused at his interest. He seldom remembered now that he'd had a job with a carpet company to help with the expenses of his education, or how he used to joke that between carpet-laying and seminary he spent most of his life on his knees. The entomologists had indeed hung their "Napping, Do Not Disturb" sign on their doorknob. It was hand lettered neatly on the cardboard from a shirt, and not a recent shirt from the looks of it. Snug as two bugs in a rug, Herbert thought fondly.

And then he was in the walkway from C to D, and no putting it off any longer, the sharp edge of ammonia, the whiff of fecal ripeness, the cries of rage and grief. A foretaste of heft, he thought, and all of Goldengroves swaying on the lip of it. He went on with his prayers: *That it may please thee to strengthen such as do stand; to comfort and help the weak-hearted; to raise up those who fall; and finally to beat down Satan under our feet, we beseech thee to hear us, good Lord.* Though four patients had been redistributed to other wings, a good productive six remained. No, more like a dozen, for here the rooms were single with a bath, a second room for study or sociability no longer needed; indeed, doors had been broken through walls to house the arrivals from other wings in something like their former style, though the vinyl flooring remained. He picked his way past wheelchairs to the nurse's station. Poor Donald! Poor Leonie, even, at a stretch. The trustees had not thought this through.

"I'm looking for Don Arnold," Herbert said. "I thought he might like a little visit."

"Doubtless he would," said the nurse, "but I haven't seen him since lunch.

You might check the dining room."

The dining room stank of bottom-line and good-enough, as well as things more tangible; the floor would want sweeping (or mopping, or possibly shoveling, depending on which table one looked under) before dinner. In the center of the largest table's Formica top, Professor Arnold made himself as small as possible, flinching back as Leonie banged the circumference with her wheelchair.

"Get me a stick!" she cried when she saw Herbert. "At lunch he pass the salad to everyone else but me. This art man treats me like dirt! But I still love the art of Europe, I still love Raphael and Rubens, those men knew how to treat women."

"We didn't HAVE any damn salad," Donald said to Herbert. "Can't you get her away from here? I don't dare get down. She'll go for me."

"I'll take her to her room," Herbert said. "Then you and I can have coffee at my place." She's not much crazier than she ever was, even if she imagined the salad, he thought as he pushed her chair into the corridor remembering the infamous day at the college when she had dented five, yes five, of her colleague's parked cars and called it their fault. The problem was giving her wheels again, she can get around too fast in this thing. What a ranting, bedridden tyrant she would have been once! How did we ever get used to her?

"So that's my life," Donald said into the bottom of his second cup of coffee, "and I can't see that it's in any way worth living." His trousers were still rolled up to exhibit the damages inflicted by Leonie and her wheelchair battlebot. Cuts and scars stood out against the dark cloud of old bruises.

That was Herbert's opening to say, "Of course it is," or "Now, now," but he was an honest man. He saw no hope to offer. "Oh, Donald," was what he settled on at last. And then, "Isn't there any place you can go and get away from her?"

"There are no locks on the doors of D Wing," said Donald, "no, not even on the bathroom door. She looks for a chance to roll in and expose me and jeer. I won't tell you the things she's said." Remembering them, he lost control of his voice. "I can't use my own bathroom," he wept, "I can't go, I get so anxious. I tried to hit the toilet with my back against the door to hold her out, and let me tell you that I could have done it once but it does not work out well for old men. The nurses made an awful fuss. I have to use the public washroom to do my business, those doors lock, but when I come out she's waiting as often as not and runs me down. Twice she's knocked me over. She howls at me like a pack of Furies. I'm afraid to sleep for fear I'll wake up with her teeth in my neck. I wish my mother had drowned me like a kitten." He blew his nose. "Sorry, Herbert."

"How can we make your life any better?" Herbert asked.

"I'd do anything to get back to A Wing," Donald said. "Or even if she went back and I didn't—could you ask? Isn't there anybody you could swap for me?"

Herbert was already taking stock. It would have to be Glenda or Lily, probably Glenda. She had arrived in better shape than Lily, but she seemed to grow more strange while Lily showed occasional signs of resurgence. But whom would he petition? The trustees would be insulted at any lack of satisfaction, the politics were delicate. Almost certainly Silas would block the deportation of Glenda, to whom he had been showing a certain protective deference—it was Herbert's habit to notice such things, and he knew Silas of old; Silas might even say that if they brought back Donald they must restore Leonie as well, which would squelch the attempt. WWJD, Herbert thought crankily, let those cocksure evangelical teenyboppers with their bracelets come solve this one.

His irreverence brought its own punishment: he saw at once What Jesus Would Do, and knew at the same moment that Herbert Christmas, retired chaplain and lover of luxury, lacked the spiritual resolve to carry it off. He should offer to trade with Donald, he should take the wretched man's place on D. He could handle Leonie if he had to. But oh, the easy access that all the raving and ravelling would have to his quarters, the lack of locks! The lost comfort of his little study with its rugs and books, his kitchenette. The horror, the horror, of the dining room. Had he loved Donald even a little it might have weighed against his deep love of ease, but no, he could not take that sufferer's place in hell. Small wonder that God seemed for so long to have stayed out of touch.

"I'll look into it," he murmured, "complications, ways and means. I'd try Bag Balm on those cuts."

"Never mind," said Donald, "I knew you couldn't help, really. I'm beyond saving. Thanks for letting me talk, though." He blew his nose again, rolled down his pants legs, and limped away.

"Nobody," Herbert said faintly at his back, "is beyond saving."

Except maybe me, he thought.

*

From Chelsea's notebook: What the hell went on this afternoon I wonder. Some skinny old guy I never saw before was limping down the hall crying and when I went past the old minister's door his face was wet too and he shut his door and locked it loud. I didn't know a lock could be so loud. And then it sounded like he'd hit the door with his head, thunk like a soccer ball. If they weren't so old I'd think they had a break-up fight, ick. Nobody said a thing about it. Everyone just acted normal. Like, normal for here.

THE WHEELS OF THE BUS

A clear December morning and not too cold. Orin reckoned as he pulled the Grove's smaller bus around to the main entrance that whatever might screw up the outing to Ellsworth (and the possibilities were rich), it wouldn't be the weather. Christmas shopping in Ellsworth was a ritual at the Groves. In the past, of course, nobody had mentioned the outing to the D-Wing folks, who were given by the staff and ostensibly by one another such useful reminders of decay as body lotion and bed socks, but this year they could not be left out, for gift- exchange names were drawn wing by integrated wing.

"So it seems that mainstreaming is good for somebody besides us," Millie observed to Beth.

"Orin has liked it all along," Beth said, but was too kind to say why. The small bus, which Orin was qualified to drive, could hold two wings' worth of people—today A and B—provided that there weren't too many wheelchairs. A trip to Bangor would have offered more choices but it was farther and thus more complicated; Ellsworth, rich in gift shops for the summer trade, served well enough. The two couples, who by some sleight of hand better unexamined, had managed to draw one another's names, would themselves be driving to Bangor on another day, a proper getaway with shopping, a meal out, possibly even a real movie, something with a strong plot and no ducks. Today they were on the bus not only to help Chelsea and Kelly with the wheelchairs but to help some of the wheelchairs' occupants in the exercise of coherent thought.

Even Silas and Thatcher, who often drove themselves places, came along every year. It was, at least, something to do.

"Going home?" suggested an erstwhile D-Winger now living on B.

"Just going on a little spree, Sadie," said Millie as she steadied her up the steps.

"Ah," said Sadie. "Home."

"Don't worry about it," said one of the B-wingers. "She thinks she's going home when they take her to the dining room. She won't remember."

Partway to Ellsworth Kelly whispered to Chelsea, "Shouldn't we have made them sing? People always sing on bus trips."

"Oh God," said Chelsea, "don't you remember the party? Well at least let them pick. This bunch will adjourn the meeting before they'll sing about the wheels of the bus going round and round."

"Fine," said Kelly, a little hurt. "I think they guy behind us taught music."

"Yes, leave it to me, girls," he said, and hummed a stanza. Heads turned.

"What the hell language is that?" Chelsea whispered. "And why do they all seem to know the words?"

Many of them did indeed know the words, or at least knew Latin and were pleased to hear it again, or at any rate remembered Mario Lanza's performance of it in *The Student Prince*, which they were the right age to have seen. "Gaudeamus igitur Iuvenes dum sumus," they sang as the bus rolled through the wintery landscape. Sebastian turned around to translate. "'Therefore let us rejoice while we're young.' It's an old student drinking song." He never stumbled when he was quoting.

But you're NOT fucking young!" the girls screamed inwardly, but by then the busload was singing "Post molestam senectutem/ Nos habebit humus."

"After troublesome old age the earth will hold us,"

Sebastian supplied with a little smile. He knew what they were thinking. He took up the song again: "Ubi sunt qui ante nos/ In mundo fuere?" 'Where are those who were in the world before us?'" And we know the answer to that, he said to himself, savoring the taste of mummy.

Gaudeamus Igitur was a rousing success, though most singers lost confidence after the first verse or two. Never mind, they hummed along or sang the first stanza again. They beat time on their knees. The music professor knew all seven stanzas, and so did Sebastian. Silas and Millie knew most of them; possibly the words were locked in Harlow as well, for when Millie said to him, "We like this one, don't we, Harlow?" he nodded and beamed. They sang it through several times and rolled down into Ellsworth's main shopping street still caroling that life was brief and would soon be finished. "Vita nostra brevis est/ Brevi finietur." Sebastian decided not to give the girls any details about the bad manners of death. They didn't need to know yet that Nemini parcetur, nobody is spared.

Disembarked, for a few moments, they all paused on the sidewalk, waiting for the others to declare their directions, wishing to avoid not only those for whom they were buying, but those who might be buying for them. "Where to?" whispered Chelsea, who could feel herself getting into the spirit of it. "Candy store," hissed Lily, "I've got Herbert Christmas." They set off for the nearest crosswalk, and Beth followed with Glenda, who could so far state no preferences. Silas headed for the bookstore. *Pilgrim's Progress*? thought Sebastian, imagining by what literary means Silas, if he had his name, might try to reform him, but Bunyan was more his own period than Silas's, so perhaps not.

What Sebastian hoped to find for Thatcher was some concrete encouragement for his penile recreations. Jam would be possible, jam in bright colors, marmalade with its jeweled scraps of rind, a follow-up for the butter experiment which once again had produced too little effect, though Sebastian had seen Herbert Christmas looking at it with some interest. Herbert would have looked with interest at anything buttered, Sebastian imagined, and he hoped that the addition of jam would not undo him. Oh for the sex shops of yore, he thought; body paint would have been the ticket. He strolled across the street to a shop that specialized in local goods, where he acquired a small jar of pickled fiddleheads for himself and a larger jar of blackberry jam for Thatcher. It was a start. As he left, Beth was wheeling Glenda in and heading for the soap. Both women, for different reasons, were alight with interest.

Finger paints? mused Sebastian. Would finger paints work on human skin? He crossed the street once again to visit the toy store and nearly bumped into Thatcher himself, who was swinging a shopping bag. Thatcher was smiling. He had gone over budget to buy Lily a pink leather squid, a hand puppet that trailed tentacles of ribbons like a maypole. "Or would that be merpole?" Thatcher joked to himself, feeling good and wondering whether ribbons would be a worthwhile addition to his own display.

In the bookstore, Silas, who had indeed drawn Sebastian's name, was scanning the literary paperbacks for something annoying but salutary, or better, annoying AND salutary. He was sorry to find himself rejecting the most acidic of the choices, but Sebastian, however deplorable, had since his Thankfulness maneuver seemed an antagonist who might require more skillful handling than Silas had reckoned. Sebastian would not take well to any sort of obvious reproof; he would retaliate. In the end, Silas chose a Sixties reader with a peace symbol on the cover—Burroughs, Bruce, Cleaver, Friedan, Steinem, and so on, not all that peaceful surely. Sebastian had evidently enjoyed the Sixties, as he himself most bitterly had not. But Silas had an inkling that what Sebastian had liked was the color and energy, the free love, perhaps the easy drugs, not so much the literature. If so, rereading it, Sebastian might sense a lack of quality and regret his past. It was the worst that Silas dared to do. At the checkout counter he saw Harlow holding *Great Love Songs of the Twentieth Century*, music for that wrong headed wife of his. He wondered who had Glenda's name.

Elsewhere on the street Glenda herself was buying a gift for Silas. Though Beth, by way of experiment, had tried to suggest any number of other things, Glenda had been unable to leave the soap display for long. The colors, the curves, the scents! When had she seen such riches? Oh, she wanted them all.

Why must she share it with Silas? At last she settled on a box of bath-sized soap scented with balsam, such a pretty green. Beth, who could hardly wait to tell Millie about Glenda, thought it likely that if the soap ever got to Silas it would soon disappear again. "Very suitable," she told Glenda, "cleanliness is next to godliness," and choked on a swallowed giggle. At that very moment, in another shop, Herbert Christmas was buying Glenda red soap shaped like roses. He too had identified the A-Wing raider of bathrooms, but unlike Beth and Millie he was trying to hold her in charity even as he wrapped his personal soap in a handkerchief and hid it in the jacket pocket of his best suit.

Sebastian, who had lingered to consider current trends in decoration (everything bigger and shinier than in his childhood), was one of the last to arrive at the bus. High on the sheer excess of it all, he longed to chatter and had an urge to wink at Thatcher, but he was firm with himself. It was pleasure enough to remember that in his second parcel was a children's kit for face painting. Faces, or whatever.

*

From Chelsea's notebook: What a day. I was actually lucky to have Lily, she's not as crazy as she looks, but Kelly was really upset on the bus. She had to fight with a salesclerk to let old Sadie in the wheelchair use the store bathroom before it was too late and then she had to help her get on the john and the room was really small. I said we could all sing "Grandma Got Run Over By A Reindeer" if it would make her feel better, but she didn't think it was furuly. She's so grossed out by seeing Sadie's wrinkled old ass that she wants to quit. When I got home I said to my boyfriend "Gowdyamus igetar" and he said "Baby!" and grabbed me. Afterwards he said what was that gowdyiger thing you said? And I said never mind, it's a long story, just use it while you got it, is all, the nose hair comes next, but why did you grab me if you didn't know what it meant? Because I still got it, he said, and smiled that cute evil smile of his. I'm thinking let me die before forty, that's old enough.

TICKLE ME, SILAS

Silas had gone to spend Christmas with his elder sister Nancy in Portsmouth. Many, even most, people found Nancy a cranky, bean-counting little pickle of a woman, but she and Silas got on very well. Irritable, they did not irritate one another. They indulged together in cocoa, cribbage, and familiar movies. They share a disapproval of modern frivolity, save that Nancy failed to hate canned music, or at least to hate it enough, while Silas, though he tried for Nancy's sake, felt insufficient umbrage towards new shades in roses. Their childhood had been formal and wholesome: they had addressed their parents as Mother and Father, saved their nickels in special banks, won (and worn) Sunday. School medals for perfect attendance, and been forbidden to whine. They had not resented this regimen until, a dozen years after Silas's birth, their sunny brother Jeremy was born into a different childhood entirely. He called their parents Mom and Pop, swiped sugar from the bowl, laughed at his elders, and was adored by everyone except his siblings. Jerry always landed on his feet. They had waited in vain for moral laxness to bring him down, cosmic retribution; even a childless first marriage and amicable divorce that been repaired by a brand new marriage to a woman with four children. Thus Jerry, no surprise, reaped where he had not sown. It was enough, they felt, to make responsible people cross and, trusting one another, they said as much over their cocoa.

And now Silas was being driven back to the Groves in his own car by Nancy, who would deliver him like a package and take the bus home. A folded wheelchair, his for six weeks, rattled in the trunk, and although the pain of his broken right ankle and dislocated left hip was dulled by drugs, he burned with outrage. None of it was fair.

"We spoiled their day, I suppose," he said to Nancy.

"Least we could do," said Nancy with more than usual bile. "Old and young should never have to mix."

Not if it ends this way, Silas thought. A wheelchair! How could a man at eye level with shirt buttons and belts maintain a moral advantage? And oh dear, the women!

Neither he nor Nancy had been thrilled by their brother's invitation to come up to Portland for Boxing Day and meet the new wife and children.

Showing off, they had both thought at once, single and childless as they were; attributing low motives to Jeremy was comforting, as any suspicion of charity was not. "You'll find us in considerable chaos," Jerry had said with his usual cheer, "what with the children and all their Christmas toys, but we'll have a nice roast of beef, this girl of mine is some cook, and it's time the kids met their Auntie Nancy and Uncle Silas." Silas could imagine too well how he and his sister would look to those children—prissy, withered, and older than dirt.

Silas believed himself to love children—his whole educational philosophy rested on a conviction of early innocence—but had he looked at his feelings more closely he might have seen that he felt about the very young much of the unease that he had felt about the occupants of D Wing. He did know, and regretted, that every year of a childless life made the very young more alien. At thirty he might have gingerly sat a child upon his knee. At fifty he could still open a conversation, however vapid. Now he could only look at them and smile benignly; anything more had to be initiated by the child itself.

It did not appear than his new nieces and nephews would be shy. Jeremy, one arm around a wife so young and pretty that she made him look old, called them over and said, "Okay, gang, I want you to meet your Aunt Nancy and your Uncle Silas." Four children who seemed at a guess to be ten, seven, five, and three wandered up to inspect their sudden relatives. "Nancy, Silas," he went on, "meet Lance, Mariana, Harry, and Christabel." Lance shook hands and Christabel giggled. The other two gazed with mild impassive interest.

"Merry Christmas," said Silas, and "Happy Boxing Day," said Nancy.

They each produced (as they had jointly agreed would be suitable) a five-dollar bill for each child, and the children, lately sated with toys, seemed warmed by the unexpected bonus. "Would you like to see our new toys?" they offered, and Jeremy's wife said, "After dinner. Now go wash your hands." It was all most promising.

Over roast beef and Yorkshire pudding, Jeremy explained that his wife, Yvonne, was a great anglophile, that she had spent a study-abroad year at Chester, that she had been, as he knew Silas would appreciate, an English major. Ah well, thought Silas, that accounted for the names: Sir Lancelot, Mariana at the Moated Grange, King Harry, and Coleridge's unfortunate heroine. Wasn't Yvonne bothered that things had not turned out entirely well for some of the names' previous owners?

"Ah," he said, "no wonder the children have such literary names." Yvonne beamed. "I told Jerry you'd appreciate those," she said.

"Christabel, watch your gravy; Harry, your Yorkshire pudding is not a toy, don't bounce it."

"All this," said Jeremy, "and beauty too. Am I a lucky man or what?" "Always have been, Jerry," said Silas through his teeth.

"You're all too kind," said Yvonne. "Take a drink of water, Mariana; I warned you about the horseradish. No, Lance, your sister is not an idiot; she just made a little mistake. Everyone okay now?"

Still, Silas reckoned, none of them had uttered terrible oaths or fallen off their chairs or coughed up their beef, which put this holiday dinner way ahead of festivities at the Groves. So far these seemed to be rather nice children. Even Herbert Christmas would have admired this dinner: they were having two trifles for dessert, one laced with sherry for the grown-ups, the other with orange juice for the children. Yvonne had put a snowman on the latter so no mistakes could be made. How pretty the trifles were in their stemmed bowls, all the layers showing through the glass! The children, Yvonne explained, had never really taken to Christmas pudding, except once when the holly on top had caught fire and spit sparks, so she had given up on that Dickensian touch.

"Don't you wish our folks could have seen this," Jeremy said to Nancy and Silas. "They always hoped for grandchildren, you know, and we all let them down." No we don't wish it, you utterly utterly tackless lout! his elders thought in sync, or that was the gist of it. They could not have borne it if Jeremy had given their parents this too, along with the gift of his sunny informal self. Silas tried to swallow his pique with his trifle and could see that Nancy was doing something similar. Their sullen eyes met.

All done?" said Yvonne at last. "Jerry and I will clear up. Why don't you guys take your uncle and aunt into the living room now and show them your things," and suddenly Silas found himself borne along like a wad of paper in a flooded gutter. A small gravy-slick hand seized his forefinger and steered him to a chair, while Mariana installed Nancy in another. All the bright chaos of modern toydom lay piled and tangled at their feet.

The children burrowed and wallowed, arose clutching favorites.

Christabel, who had taken to Silas, leaned against his knees and thrust towards him something red and shaggy. "Tickle Me Elmo!" she cried. Is she calling me Elmo? he thought, but before he could embarrass himself by saying it, she had punched the creature three times and it had, apparently, gone into a fit, twitching and shrieking. Christabel shrieked along with it, and Silas hoped that he and Elmo had not twitched together. Where were the teddy bears of yesteryear? He saw Mariana waving a small egg-shaped object at Nancy, who was saying in pained tones, "What did you call it, Dear? But how can it have waste to clean? Where would it, ah, come out?" Mariana appeared to be answering, through her laughter, in Japanese.

With a whoop of sirens, Lance's remote-controlled

police car made for Silas's chair. "Watch THIS, Uncle Silas!" Lance bellowed. "Elmo's for girls!" Silas lifted his feet just in time, as Christabel shrilled "Elmo is a boy himself, you poopyhead!" A labyrinth of yellow tracks coiled and humped behind her.

"Is that your race track, Harry?" Silas asked.

"It's all of ours," Harry said, and pop went a nerf-gun projectile; a ball ricocheted from the ceiling. "We can shoot at the ceiling but not at the Christmas tree or each other," he explained. "We aren't supposed to break things or people."

"Quite right," Silas agreed, thinking Ye Gods, haven't they heard of outdoors?

But Harry had moved on to his aunt, clearing a path for a robot who strolled, Simon thought, with excessive confidence for a piece of fancy plastic, swinging his arms and turning his head from side to side like a crown prince. Silas could tell from Nancy's alarmed expression that the thing had addressed her, but he couldn't hear over the car's siren and Elmo's hysterics what it had said. Could it have made an improper suggestion? He put nothing, absolutely nothing, beyond the godless toys of the century's end. Nancy shrank from it, as she would no doubt have done if it had merely said, "Good morning" or "Feed me," but weren't the children laughing too hard for that? Should he contrive a way to rescue his sister? And there was Mariana at his left elbow with a jar of purple glop, into which she was plunging her fingers. The glop farted with horrible realism, which was apparently its purpose. When were their parents coming back? Had they taken the chance to slip off alone? How long had he and Nancy been listening to the toys, and the children, whoop and giggle and fart? It felt like hours.

Now Christabel was rolling on the floor in front of him, demanding "Tickle me, Silas!" and cracking herself up. "Tickle me, Silas; tickle me, Silas," she chortled, and her energy showed no need of recharging.

"Tickle me, Silly-ass," Lance whispered to Mariana, "Uncle Silly-ass."

Silas, who could hear him, thought that the boy was right; though his language was disgustingly vulgar: he had been silly to come to Jeremi's place. He and Nancy could have been in their slippers watching "It's a Wonderful Life" and it would have been.

Across the chaos Nancy had the boneless look of

her childhood's rag doll companions who had kept a wise silence and demanded nothing. He stood up to go to her, planning to make some excuse to Jeremy and Yvonne, when Lance's police car clipped him on the ankle and he staggered. Staggering, he stepped wide to avoid Christabel, who had inconveniently sat up. "Don't step on Elmo!" she cried, and he tried to shift again. No man his age could have done that dance and stayed upright. He felt himself falling like a tree, arms out too late, and saw the yellow tracks just before he flattened them. "Our race tracks!" a high voice lamented and a nerf ball bounced off his backside.

"Uncle Silly-Ass has hurt himself," Mariana said soberly. "Somebody better find Mom."

Epiphany Weather

The weather oracles promised something out of the ordinary, and Thatcher was pleased. A big storm would kindle his spirits, which suffered in part from the conventional post-Christmas slump and in part from a malaise peculiar, as far as he know, to himself. Epiphany, with its conflation of kings and scholars, made him feel bareheaded. The painted Magi, robed and crowned, glittered on their way to their stellar conclusion, as wise men should. What jokes soever he had made to the contrary, Thatcher adored an academic procession. At the opening bars of "Pomp and Circumstance" his chin went up and his stride lengthened. He relished the pull of his academic hood against his shoulders and the way his shabbiest colleagues burst into color. But when he thought of the Magi, no bullion-tasseled mortarboard, no, not even the puffy velvet hat of Cambridge, seemed crown enough.

Rain, said the oracles, and freezing cold, and rain again, and then some. It didn't sound all that spectacular—Thatcher had once narrowly escaped a typhoon—but the announcer sounded nervous. Nervous was good. All their cupboards were full of Christmas booze and snacks, so let it come. They were old enough, and concentrated enough, that pretty soon some agency would be making sure they weren't dead. The first forty-eight hours of bad weather were unimpressive, in his opinion, though the roads were murder. Books and bridge grew oddly tiresome. Newspapers were hard to come by. Television still worked, but the habits of their generation and their jobs had kept it peripheral in their lives. Silas became more bossy, Sebastian more silent. Glenda rolled all the way to B Wing and came back with her pockets aromatic and bulging.

During dinner on the fourth night of foul weather, while Thatcher was gazing into the darkness and spooning in beef stew with automatic hand, a tree not far from the window came down with a crash. "Whoa," said Thatcher to Silas, "did you see that?"

"See what, Thatcher?" said Silas in his most irritating tone, one that suggested long-suffering inadequately disguised as patience.

"The goddam tree fell right over," said Thatcher. "I am sure it didn't," said Silas.

"It damned well did," said Thatcher. "Didn't any-body else see it?" Harlow was nodding and exclaiming; he'd seen it too.

"Oh good," said Lily. "I thought I'd imagined it."

Sebastian and Beth and Orin crowded into the win-dow. "It was all covered in ice," said Beth.

"Heavy, very heavy," Sebastian agreed, "heavy." "Shallow root system," Orin added.

"Let's take our cake to the lounge," said Millie. "The windows are better there." The cake that night, choc-olate with raspberry-jam filling, would become for a short time a shared memory of the normal.

"Ah, jam," Thatcher said to Sebastian and winked. Sebastian laughed. He could at least laugh like other people, he was pleased to note. One hoot is a lot like another, he could keep it up forever and not be pegged for repetition. He would have to laugh more.

Settled down with the lights turned out they ate their cake in small bites and watched nature, which was putting on one hell of a show. "Oooh," they said, and "Aaah," like people at a fireworks display. At the same time, they deplored the wreck of the trees; even Silas was pro-tree, though he preferred the sculptured evergreens of Italian landscape. Their cries were partly dismay.

For Harlow they were mostly dismay: the detonation of branches breaking reminded him too much of his war experience, which he had put some effort into forgetting. "Wug," he said to Millie hoarsely, and she explained to the others, "It's the war, Harlow had shell shock when he got back from France and some things just remind him." The others nodded. They were all familiar with that brand of post-traumatic stress. Even Silas, who'd been too young to go, was remembering a colleague who had once dived under his desk when the lights flickered. There arose in all of them the unspoken reflection that it was nice to be with people who understood which conflict "the war" was. They had more or less adapted to students whose war was Vietnam, but many had suffered a kind of temporal crisis the first time they heard a student say "Of course I'm too young to remember the war" and mean Southeast Asia.

"Tree!" cried Glenda as a willow toppled and hit the ground with a whump and rattle. "Ooh," said the others. As more trees fell, their excitement grew and their sensibilities numbed. Intent at the window, they merely kept score: "Big one," "Small one," "Right across the driveway." In the intervals they spoke of trees they had known.

"I fell out the neighbors' pear tree and broke my arm," said Herbert Christmas.

"Harlow and I had such beautiful birches behind our first little house, didn't we dear," Millie said.

"Birches!" Beth said. "They'll never be straight again."

Orin considered telling about the time his dad, who used to cut a switch to whip him when he needed it, got so mad he came at him with a whole bush, and they all laughed so hard that he wasn't whipped after all. But like the things he was thankful for, it was nobody's business.

"I had a tree house," said Thatcher, "where I could get away. Kept me out of trouble."

"Mine was a spot under the lilac bush," Lily said. "I hid there when I was already in trouble."

Silas, who had grown up in Hartford, remembered no intimacy with trees for either good or ill, and it made him cross. Jeremy no doubt had found himself a friendly tree somewhere. These people were having far too much fun. "What have we done to deserve this punishment," he groused. His question was met with a widespread cynical whoop. Game shows, pesticides, plagiarism, they tossed into the kitty, their eyes on the windows, Hawaiian punch, coveting our neighbor's asses, Newt Gingrich. Herbert Christmas cut them off. "I hope you don't really take this for divine punishment, Silas," he remarked. "Nature is nature, it goes its own way."

Before Silas could mount a rebuttal, someone cried, "Look at that!" and with fresh shock they watched a utility pole sway and hang and then crash, dragging its wires down with it. The lights of Goldengroves went out. There were squeaks from those whom squeaks would not unman.

They went on watching. Watching: Sebastian heard the old funereal undertone in the word. One watched with the dead or dying. Was the world outside the Groves in mortal peril? A feeling crept over the group in the lounge that these people would not be much worse to die with than any others. Even Silas. Even Glenda the soap bandit. They were almost glad to be together, and glad, to their embarrassment, that in a group they were less likely to be overlooked. But after all, it was only a storm.

With a great flash the horizon went electric blue. Second and third flashes farther away, followed.

"I think Harlow and I will leave you now," said Millie. "Don't worry, we can find our way by counting doors." "What is it?" said Lily, enchanted.

The first lines of a friend's poem rose up in Sebastian's head: "It was the Chinese first, to no one's great surprise, who devised a way to hurl fire through the skies." He did so hope this was NOT the Chinese.

"Northern Lights?" ventured Silas.

"No," said Thatcher, "I've seen the Northern Lights. They undulate more."

Orin was laughing inside. Trust professors not to know anything practical. "It's the transformers blowing up," he said. "I believe we' re in for quite a spell of darkness."

COLD

O n the second night that the power was out, the dark came early. They ate soup brought by the National Guard and took to their beds for the sake of warmth. Fully dressed, in layers, with their blankets and quilts and afghans around them, A Wing contemplated coldness.

Thatcher thought first about windigoes, about the giant cannibals with icy hair who snap trees in their paths with a crack like those he could hear outside. He imagined a Cree family tense in their winter quarters, hearing such sounds in the forest, reading them as outsize footsteps getting closer, wondering if they'd be the windigo's choice for dinner. Was it so different from British families huddled in Anderson shelters, counting the space between bombs, knowing the next one might be theirs? Huddling and waiting for death, cold or hot, was that the common thread in human culture? And now he'd never have a class to shock with such a notion; that was the hell of wisdom in old age—your captive audience was gone. Turning his mind to brighter things, he set himself to remember the many verses of "Eskimo Nell," the popular and infamous ballad of Deadeye Dick, Mexican Pete, and the world's most formidable hooker. If he lost a rhyme he could supply his own; "Eskimo Nell" was always in flux. It was the last stanzas he dwelt on, Nell's boast of the superiority of sex in the frozen north with its six-month nights, where even the dead slept two in a bed, everything was hard, and "spunk" rhymed with "chunk." He added some verses: Nell in Maine, Nell in the ice storm. He was entertained.

Sebastian remembered flying into Juneau in his wartime days as a cargo pilot, Juneau, where it was so cold that people in the street constantly brushed their hands across their noses to test for feeling. In his unheated cockpit he would count the minutes until he landed, hoping he'd still be functional. One day, the coldest of days, he wasn't, he couldn't move his hands from the controls to open the door, he thought they'd find his body still at its post. That could have happened, would have if he hadn't managed to hit the communication switch with his knee and call for help. They got him out and thawed him. Even if the power was out for a week it would be nothing compared to that. But of course he too was nothing compared to his young and hot-blooded self. To every age its sufficient threat.

Orin thought of ice fishing, not of the sport itself but of those who'd broken through and gone down to the bottom of the lake, where they were cold forever. His Uncle Lee's old '38 International pickup truck was down there and his Uncle Lee had gone with it, he hadn't gotten out in time or couldn't find his way up, they never knew. He'd been a fool to go on the ice with no pal but his dog, not a soul to tell his story, and now their bones turned in the currents of frigid water. Right after the war, that must have been, when it was easier to get gas, so he must have been what, ten, when he heard it. He seemed to have seen it all his boyhood, the crack and plunge, then silt drifting up in clouds from where the tires settled on the bottom. He had never let himself imagine the part in between and he didn't intend to start now. It was the dog that broke his heart, Old Carlo they'd called him. Orin himself had ice fished in his teens and twenties but he'd never liked it. Against all logic he'd feared to hook a sodden cap, a mitten, a bone nibbled clean by lake fish.

There were tales of the drowned in Beth's island childhood too, but today it was the wind from Charleston Hill that blew across her memory. The piercing cold of the walk back to the dorm after study hall, when even a boyfriend's hand in yours was not warmth enough, when pausing to kiss was sometimes not as good as getting inside a heated building two minutes earlier. This was in the days before down jackets, layered hoodies, micro fleece, when you wore your wool coat and maybe a scarf looped once around your head, and you counted on your hot blood to keep you thawed and you'd die before you'd wrap up like an old lady. A lot of the island kids went to mainland boarding schools, if they were smart enough to educate, but they all missed the ocean, they missed the look of the sky and the different quality of cold. Inland there was too much snow and the wind had a meaner bite. She knew that she'd liked Higgins Classical, that she'd felt she was seeing something of the larger world. She'd had good friends. Now and then she'd found herself in love. Sometimes in dreams she recaptured the heat of adolescence and would think just as she woke that she was in her old dormitory bed, but why was she wearing her mother's body? So her

Higgins years must be stored in her head entire, and yet memory tonight brought her only the cold, the snow drifts, the wind in her face.

Like Orin, Lily thought of water, not the tropical water of her fantasies nor yet the lake water of his nightmares, but the icy Atlantic where the codfish lived. Would she never get them out of her head? Gadus morhua, eaten around the world, dried, salted, boiled, and rolled into balls, but dull, dull, dull. How did it feel to be a codfish, to swim in a pack, to eat without choice whatever drifted into its ever open mouth? To die without protest, limp on the hook, resigned, a dead weight? Was it glad to give up its gelid life in the shoals? Was there any animal in nature less like herself than a codfish? Or herself as she had been, as she really was inside. Perhaps now she, Lily, had become like a codfish too, living in groups, eating whatever was given her, no longer put off by the idea of death.

Millie thought of winter on Moosehead Lake; the snap of branches reminded her of ice breaking up in the spring. But before that happened, all the long winter, they had walked to school on the high banks of plowed snow, looking down at cars, playing giants. Sometimes a punky spot would swallow a leg to its boot top. Snow froze to ice in their overshoes' ugly buckles, which had to be pried open in the cloakroom with chilled fingers. In the cloakroom, too, on the coldest days their dinner pails froze, mason jars of milk bursting and spoiling the food, and then the other children, the ones with thermoses, shared their sandwiches. How she had longed to be a boy and wear high gum-rubber boots indoors and out! She moved closer to Harlow.

Harlow was glad she had. He had been remembering the Forest of Ardennes in the winter of '44. They had slept on the ground when they slept at all, their coats wet and stiff. It was the coldest place in the world, where spilled blood turned solid on the skin. The wounded froze to death and the snow went on falling and dusted their bodies, piling up in the folds of their uniforms. You saw then that they'd turned to things, inanimate as stones, and he had yet to see a sight more pitiful than that. His boys, only in their teens, most of them, the very air around them lethal with splinters and shrapnel—he worried all the time, or so it seemed now, but the worry must have been an underground current, because you couldn't think for the shelling. It was the cold and the cracks like gunshot that had brought Ardennes back to him, he supposed. Would the trees around The Groves look like a war zone tomorrow? Some men treasure war in retrospect for its intensity, but Harlow thought it had been the most wretched time of his life; even the lyrics to "Lili Marlene" could fill him with a black misery like poison gas. Men had called it the Ghost Front with greater aptness then they knew.

Herbert Christmas considered the phrase "till hell freezes over." A frozen hell more apropos, perhaps, than the fiery pit. Cold bit and burned too, it got into your bones, and wasn't it a better representation of a place abandoned by God, a world without the warmth of divine love? His mind filled with icy images of tombs cut in rock from whose opening no stones had been rolled away, of Decembers with no solstice. He had been punished by cold when as a child he had given away his mittens to Bobby Sawyer, whose fingers were blue, and hadn't dared to tell his mother. Once at seminary he'd offered up his jacket when a beggar, for a flickering moment, had looked like Jesus; his roommate had lent him an old coat and told him he'd had a true vision. Had his roommate been right? Once upon a time, he thought, he'd discerned his Lord in the bread and wine, though not every Sunday. The last discerning had been a long time back.

Now he yearned for hot toast and jam. He prayed that it was not the food itself, but food as the gift of seasons and sun, sustenance as the bounty of a radiant god. He prayed that some connection between his life and his faith had merely shaken loose, that he was not, after all, caught in the dark and frigid night of the soul.

Glenda, whose memory worked better the farther back it went, had pulled her top blanket around her neck and was thinking of the Franklin Expedition, that doomed Victorian attempt to discover the Northwest Passage. She had written a term paper on it long ago, and as well as she could remember she'd gotten an A. And that, she added to herself, was before A's became cheap. The Erebus. The Terror. Who, she had always wondered, would have willingly embarked on ships with such grim names? But most she saw, tonight, the ship's crew dragging loaded longboats across the pack ice, dragging their heavy silly loads and hoping for rescue. The cold would have pierced their naval uniforms. They had brought from England no sufficient furs to keep them warm. No, but they had brought good silver, carpet slippers, a 2900-book library, a hand organ, and no doubt fancy soap. Oh fancy soap, didn't she know someone who was burdening her last trek with a long-boat full of soap? She hoped that someone would rescue that poor fool, whoever she was. But no one had rescued the Franklin Expedition, and how cold they must have been, how numbed by ice and more ice. Their minds must have clouded too, poisoned by clumsy lead solder.

The trappings of propriety did not keep them alive. They must have learned to feel old.

Silas was loving it. He sat at his window, a cocoon of blankets around his wheelchair, and gazed at the crystal world. All creation shone. He had never seen a world so clean, so opposite to smutty. It was cold, yes, and some people would die of it, perhaps some people at the Groves itself, but if the freeze lasted forever and they all died, the sight of utter purity would not have cost too high a price. He thought of Robert Frost, poet of winter, and his speculation on how the world would end, by fire or ice. Now he knew that he, Silas, preferred ice to the chaos and smudge of fire. How right to die en-cased in diamond like a fly in amber. He was seized by a great intention that all words and deeds around him should be worthy of this lucid world from which even the trees, perhaps, were being cleared away. Starting tomorrow he would roll through the dark halls, flashlight in pocket, a soldier in the army of virtue.

SINS AND ERRORS

On the third night of darkness, Sebastian sat in his reading chair but was not comforted; with the power out, his books were mute. It occurred to him that he was lonely. Self-containment in his probable decay, which had seemed to him the most honorable and least irritating course, had so far worked well enough.

Never a person who cared for groups or clubs, he reckoned that no degree of senility would find him playing Bingo or singing "The Teddy Bear's Picnic." He was, however diminished, still himself. Head and groin had been his compass points, he thought, and since his groin had slacked off he had lived in his head alone and he liked it there. His semi-seclusion at the Groves had been a natural extension of his life outside, where he had been happiest in his study, pursuing thoughts from book to book, greeting old friends, laughing at new sallies of wit. But once there had been more phone calls—too many, he had often thought—and lunches, drinks after work, just enough humanity to keep him connected, and he had been choosy about his friends.

Old age might require altered strategies.

Deeper, he was aware that in elevating the notion of Jane, he had chosen to live with a wraith. He did not regret that choice in itself; we act out of who we are, and a ghostly woman was perhaps the only kind who could have lived with him or vice versa, but he wondered now why he had not tried hard to find her. He wondered whether she was still alive. Strange to imagine her old; to him she had been youth incarnate. In the long-ago year when she had left, lost was lost unless one resorted to private detection, which would have been unseemly, but he understood that nowadays people could sometimes rather easily be found by the use of the computer. He owned a computer but had not yet made its acquaintance. Someone like the girl Chelsea might know what to do. Wouldn't it be the ultimate Silas-tease if he could bring Jane back to their lives in even the most discarnate way? If he found her, if he mastered e-mail, which must be easy enough, they could talk again, and it wouldn't matter that her appearance, her accidens, had changed, her essence would be the same. It was a thing to think about. Had his pride let her get away, his hurt at being collaterally abandoned with the worm Silas?

And was it not Pride that kept him silent and solitary now? He feared the pity or laughter— much likelier the latter in a clutch of doddering academics- that might greet his odd compulsive speech. He would have liked to go to his grave still the formidable Sebastian Antioch whose tongue was a scythe, but that it seemed, was no longer an option. He now had a tongue more like a revolving door. At least, he told himself, though Pride was the worst of the sins, it was far from the tackiest. And damn all, it had just nailed him again.

COOKOUT

The next day, Orin and Beth were restless. They weren't all that old, and they wanted to see the ice. By mid-afternoon they couldn't stand the confinement a minute longer, never mind that all the residents had been told to stay in. They put on sweaters and Macinaws, warm hats, and their grippiest boots; they sneaked out a back door like naughty giggling children. The world was amazing, all glitter and glass. The air was clean as washed linen. How had they stayed so long in the fug of elderly breath? They made a complete circuit of the Groves, hand on wall for security, crouching below sight-line at the windows. It was better than Winter Carnival at the college, with its little booths built of ice blocks. Here were ice benches, ice cars, an ice fireplace for cookouts, fallen ice trees, ice confetti from branches and wires. And on top of the shining fields the branches themselves, meshed like beaver dams, high as a human.

"Want to go camping?" said Orin. "Sleep in a little branch hut?"

Beth laughed. "No," she said, "but I do want a cook-out. Right now, today.

Look at all that fuel! Couldn't you knock the ice off the fireplace?"

"Sure," said Orin. "Back of an axe ought to do it, there's one in the tool shed. We got anything to cook?"

Millie had things to cook, a whole package of hot dogs she'd frozen just before the storm, in case the children came, and they were only just thawed. She had buns and mustard too, and Beth had butter and piccalilli. Orin had a six pack of Bud. "We'll eat at our place," Beth said, "it will make a change for you." On the branchy ends of a limb, sharpened by Harlow with his pocket knife (his Christmas gift from Orin and Beth), the hotdogs blackened and sizzled. Beth and Orin looked at one another, laughed, and knew why. They felt free and independent, fit to fend for themselves, not sit around on their aging arses and wait for someone to bring a handout. They felt as though the hotdogs were prey, something they'd caught and clubbed. They felt young. The rolls smoked and charred in spots, but what does youth care for that, and at least they'd warmed. Lunch had been cold tuna sandwiches and a fruit cup, nothing hot since coffee that morning. Beth carried the food inside, wrapped in towels, while Orin put out the fire.

"And old Silas didn't even catch me," Beth said, still laughing. She and Millie were putting dogs and rolls together fast before they could cool, two each for the girls, three for the boys. "Depity Dawg," said Millie. "Respect mah authoritah," said Beth. They were higher than hawks, and they hadn't even cracked the beer yet.

It was a feast. Around the tiny flicker of Millie's tea candle they sat in their sweaters and jackets and stuffed. Beth and Orin felt almost warm. Harlow didn't choke once, not badly. Orin belched from the beer. "Pardon me, Silas," he said. They came perilously close to singing rude songs.

"The thing is," Orin was saying half an hour later, "those professors aren't like normal people. They retire but they don't give it up. You and me, Harlow, when we quit we quit. I don't think about cleaning. You don't think about whatever the hell it was you did, am I right?" Harlow nodded with vigor.

"Harlow was a professor once, you know," Millie said. "He has a doctorate in Education, but then he went into Administration."

"Yeah," said Orin, "but you don't have a head full of it now, do you?" Though come to think of it, he said to himself, who knows what Harlow might have a head full of. He can't let on.

Harlow agreed. He mimed clapping himself on the head and finding it empty. In fact, he admitted to himself, there wasn't one hell of a lot in education to think about when you weren't actually in the classroom doing it. It was not concrete enough to cling and furnish the mind.

"But them," Orin went on, "they just keep on doing it. There's those two fools throwing quotes at each other's heads like they had a sackful, and they probably do. There's that anthropology guy running around like a native with his friggen weenie hanging out, excuse me ladies. There's the old girl who can't quit talking about codfish, for all she says she's through with it. What's the matter with them?"

For once Harlow wished he could speak. Even a Vice President who smiles a lot may harbor a sore spot or two. He would have liked to say that subject matter wasn't all they'd hung onto, that they still had a good grip on rivalry and jealousy, on showing off and jockeying for power, and that wasn't counting the ones who'd lost their wits but not their venom.

"Well, you see, dear," said Millie, "they love it so."

"I'll be gawdammed," said Orin.

DANCING WITH FEATHERS

Thatcher thought that if the power could stay off for an unprecedented three days there was no foreseeable end to it; he might as well not wait. Even by penlight, note making was possible, and he had to plan. He reckoned to stage one last spectacular indecent exposure and then give it up. If nobody reacted, he'd know he was beaten. If he got the response he looked for, he could retire with honor and turn his attention to some more promising project. Besides, he owed it to Sebastian to use his Christmas gifts, which had tickled him. He'd always liked Sebastian, in the slightly disengaged way you like people seen mostly at meetings. The guy obviously got him, appreciated the outrage, and liked new ideas. If Sebastian Antioch expected Thatcher to dip his wick in a jar of jam, what the hell, Thatcher would do it, provided he hadn't eaten all the jam to survive. As for the body paint, he was evolving some related plans.

In Niger a nomadic tribe called the Wodaabe had a passion for male beauty. Men painted their faces and danced in front of the women in beads and fancy hats. They carried mirrors. He shut his eyes and the famous photo of three Wodaabe men came back to him. He'd had that poster in grad school, he'd seen it every day for three years and he could see it still. How pretty they'd looked, tall and slim and slightly transvestite. They were hung with tassels and bells and beads; they shimmered.

And their face paint was easy enough to copy, lines from forehead to chin, constellations of beauty dots on chin and forehead. They used light colors, good on their dark skin; he would be more effective in blues and reds and greens. If his car ever thawed out he'd go to the local thrift shop for beads and headgear. He should have an ostrich feather. He still knew people in the Theatre Department, they must have one. Rising from the front of the headdress, he remembered, it was a great fluffy phallic image—in his case a mirror of, in the Nadaabe case a substitute for, the real thing. He laughed aloud. He wasn't sure how the dance went, but it didn't matter, any step would do. The Woodabe didn't expose themselves, they were gentlemen, but then, he wasn't trying out for their dance line, he was just borrowing a good publicity stunt from his nomadic brothers.

Wouldn't tonight, in the privacy of darkness, be a great time to practice a little face decoration with the help of the flashlight?

He dipped his forefinger in blue and applied a vertical line, forehead, nose, chin. A suddenly much more ethnic face gazed back from the dark mirror. Green beauty spots, perhaps; red could look like zits. He made three dots on each cheekbone, one on either side of his bisected chin. Nice. He should paint his lips black, he thought, but Goth lipstick would be preferable, if Ellsworth carried it. He tried white crescents under his eyes — more visible than he'd expected. He clapped his hands at the effect.

Oh for the friends of his wild boyhood, who would have painted too and danced with him in a line! Welt provided they were drunk enough, or else anthropologists or theatre guys. He was still eighteen inside, his knobby body was a trick of nature. He missed the invigorating company of youth. He missed the reciprocal classroom shocks that kept both him and them alive and growing. They had startled each other awake. And now his sh1dents were gone; he lived with sleepy farts and fogies. Silas! How had his department colleagues managed to teach at all, under the cloud of his disapproval?

Thatch stood up, his arms extended for balance; had anyone seen him, he would have appeared to lay his hands on the shoulders of missing friends.

Moving his feet in a little freestyle shuffle, he sang snatches of Old Man River under his breath: "I gets weary and sick of tryin', I's tired of livin' and scared of dyin'—."

Though he was not in fact scared of dying, or so he believed, the rest was true.

Everyone's Guardian Angel

The wheelchair was, after all, a good thing, Silas reflected. He knew he'd miss it when he was fully healed, which would be quite soon now. On wheels he could patrol the darkness for hours on end, flashlight at the ready. His arms seldom tired. Like all his peers, he slept in spurts and episodes; a night awake would cost him no trouble, and he savored the advantage of wakefulness while the sleepers were lost in a dark so deep. Up and down the corridors he laid his ear against closed doors, alert for sobs and retching, people in need of rescue, and flashed his light along the door cracks as a signal that help could be had if anyone cared to call out. The tired night nurse on D had said they couldn't do without him. Then, too, there might be hanky-pank afoot. Even the oldest residents, though apparently incapacitated, showed bursts of what his father had called the Old Adam. Had he known it, he and Chelsea had much the same horror of geriatric sex, and that coincidence would have made him laugh. Silas had a sense of humor, little suspected, when he was not put off his game by the unsuitable world views of others.

Rolling along, mission in mind, he nearly collided with Glenda, who had appeared as suddenly as an apparition. They stopped with their foot-rests touching. Even in the dark he thought he saw pleading in her eyes. He turned on the flashlight but held the beam a little aside.

"Miss Fessette? What's the matter?" he said. "How can I help you?" She waved a white, impatient hand. "Someone must find my husband," she said, a little imperious. "Men must be sent."

Glenda in fact had failed to clear from her mind her recent memories of the term paper on Franklin's last expedition. By now she suspected off and on that she was Lady Franklin, and the responsibility wore on her. There was something she had to do, some great weight she had to maneuver.

"I didn't know you were ever married," said Silas.

"Oh course you know," she snapped. "Don't pretend. Sir John. They call him The Man Who Ate His Boots."

"Dear Miss Fessette, Glenda," said Silas, "you are having a dream, you are in a manner of speaking sleepwalking. Let me lead you back to your room."

"Am I?" said Glenda. It seemed possible. She was very tired.

She and Silas both moved their wheelchairs back and then ahead again.

Side by side the hubs of their chairs met and caught, and for a few moments they circled together like couples at a square-dance.

"It's the committees," Glenda said vaguely, "they keep going round and round."

"There, there," said Silas, "you just hold still and I'll get us free," which in fact he quite easily did.

"Thank you for the dance," Glenda called as she rolled back into her room.

"It was my pleasure, dear lady," said Silas. And it had been.

VAGINA DENTATA MANQUEE

Lily had unfinished business in the undersea. In the more intellectually stimulating atmosphere of A Wing she had been letting her dreams slip away. She and the Giant Squid had never come together, and she wondered whether, given this night of dark idleness, she might not reenter the fluid state where she had once spent so many blissful hours. It was, at least, a thing to do. Therefore after what passed for dinner she pulled her curtains and put herself to bed, tucking under her pillow for luck the hand-puppet Thatcher had given her for Christmas. At first the gift had made her wonder what he knew, but she soon decided that she didn't care; it was a pretty toy and Thatcher was in no position to throw stones, even when he had a hand free.

Lily shut her eyes and set her mind to imagine water, water flowing around her, water lifting her, water between her face and the world. She drifted. Her hair, full and long again, trailed behind her like kelp. She was getting back. She was searching. She was available. No human had seen the mating practices of the Giant

Squid, which freed her for creativity. Her Giant Squid would be all grace in their meeting. Oh, she could make do with an octopus if the Squid stayed away, an octopus was an endearing creature, adept with its many arms, but Lily Hillman had always been an ambitious lover. Once more, then, for the high stakes, before she gave it up. Tentacles. She imagined the light stroking, the sensuous exploring tips, the more-than-human reach: one tentacle for penetration, or two perhaps, and all the others for foreplay that was not only "fore" but never ceased, sheer ongoing X-rated play. She rotated gently on her sheets. And yet there must be something missing, some feature attractive to squids that she lacked, and her mind traced the anatomy of a squid through yards of tentacle to the chittering beak at the base of the body, or what looked like the base by the standards of human anatomy. How featureless in comparison her own trunk, how soft and unpunctuated!

She removed her false teeth from her mouth—it was worth a try—and without emerging from her fantasy she bent under the covers and tried to fit them where a squid might hope for definition, a beak to clatter back at him. It would not be easy. The teeth were slippery with saliva and their shape unhandy. She did not wish to lose them past retrieval. They skidded and clacked, and then "Lily?" said Silas, and the door opened to admit his head and what appeared to be a spotlight. Her teeth squirted from her hands and disappeared between bed and wall. Silas withdrew at once with a squeak of dismay.

So, thought Lily, jerked now into full wakefulness, I guess the paparazzi have caught up at last. Where the hell are my teeth?

Silas had seen little, but that profoundly disturbing. Lily had been doing something—something!—with or to or about her private parts. At her age! This was a case for Herbert Christmas, who had earlier passed him on his way to some other emergency, on C Wing. Silas set off all abuzz to report.

Lily hung between hilarity and shame. She had actually been trying to plant her choppers in her crotch! Was she mad? And why, in the name of all the unholy hadn't she just imagined them there for the imaginary rendezvous with the imaginary squid? And Silas had caught her, Silas of all people, in his rolling Judgment Seat. Good thing the power was out, he couldn't have seen much that he understood, but what, even so, would he be saying, and to whom? She would be sorry now if she had to withdraw behind some slack-jawed mask to save her real face, for she had been liking her tentative re-entry into the human world.

The flirtation with the Giant Squid would never be consummated, and she was not altogether sorry. For a long time it had helped her escape, and thus endure, life in captivity. It had given her an aim, however grotesque. But what had she been doing to her mind? She longed for physical light to think by, so clarifying of fact and edge, so dispelling of shadows, but she would have to make do with the brief light of Silas's invasion. Her mind had been a good one, not brilliant but a good second or third-rate mind, depending on how one made one's lists. It did not deserve to have its sharpness blunted. Further, willing herself deeper and deeper into fantasy, she had been going into a kind of trance from which she might not have found the way back. Some didn't. Perhaps the Jeffrey Dahmers of the world got lost there. Perhaps child molesters, too, lay on their pillows and conjured up pale willing limbs as she had done. Though shorter. Served her right that her teeth were somewhere under the bed.

How would she distract herself now? Perhaps, she thought, she could ally herself with the teasers of Silas. She already had a spectacular start on that.

Your Old Men Will See Visions

Herbert Christmas had been having a bear of a day. It was not just the bad rations, or way his joints ached with the cold, though both wore on him. It was the people, the cranky ones who quarreled from hunger and pain and boredom, the bossy ones who expected him to make peace. Some had demanded prayers; some had wanted their hands held; some had suggested that he go to hell and take his smarmy good works with him. By twilight he might have bought a ticket and gone there if he could have been sure of a round trip. Back in his room for the moment, he added another sweater to his layers, settled into his recliner and put his feet up. There were rumors, possibly false, that a stove was now working off a generator. There was talk of casseroles involving pasta. Tuna noodle said one. Baked spaghetti, said another. Herbert thought that if these were fantasies, they were extraordinarily modest ones, not that he'd turn down hot-anything himself. But why not dream big, why not gnocchi alla Romana? He longed for winter break to be over, for the student chefs to come back and pick up their whisks. He dozed.

Rapping woke him. "Herbert?" a voice was saying, "could you get down to D Wing right away?"

"Aargh," said Herbert. "What's the trouble?"

"It's that madwoman Leonie," said the voice, which on closer examination belonged to the music professor who had led "Gaudeamus Igitur" on a bus ride that now seemed a lifetime back. "She's screaming that someone tried to kill her and nobody can shut her up."

"No wonder if they did," Herbert murmured before he was fully awake and in control of his clerical persona.

"Yeah," said the music professor. "We're all thinking about it." Leonie's screams of outrage were audible in the adjacent wings. "Goddam banshee, excuse me Herbert," observed the music prof. "Yeah," Herbert said. He was so tired.

"The sonofabitch tried to push me outdoors!" screamed the banshee. "He tried to murder me in the ice! He has never liked me! You all be glad when I'm dead! And then the coward ran away, he ran away! He knows I'll kill him back. I want Justice! Isn't this goddarn America? Where are my rights? I was young and beautiful. The sonofabitch bastard!"

"Now now," said Herbert Christmas, patting a shoulder. The arms were flailing too fast to catch. "What son of— who was it?"

'The art history man, I never bother to remember his name, he's nothing. He can't even kill right."

"That will be Doctor Arnold, Professor Donald Arnold," the nurse whispered to Herbert, "but he's such a nice man, I'm sure he wouldn't—." She looked a little wistful.

Leonie heard, all the same. "Donalarnol!" she howled. "That's not a man, it's a name for duck! I kill him myself and cook him!"

"Couldn't you give her a shot to calm her down?" Herbert whispered back. "She's liable to hurt someone. Or vice versa."

"I haven't got doctor's orders," said the nurse, "it's worth my job to do it, but I'm afraid I'll kill her myself if I don't."

"God will bless you," said Herbert.

He wondered how far to pursue the question of the missing art professor. Donald Arnold. Was he hiding and weeping somewhere in the dark corridors? Had he broken at last? Herbert, knowing his desperation, hoped that he had not walked out into the night to die of exposure like the arctic explorer Oates, but they had no one to send after him in any case. If the Guard delivered soup again tonight, perhaps they should raise the topic, but if the sufferer had found his way to the ocean it would already be too late. With Leonie drugged into silence, he and the nurse checked the missing man's room and found it empty. His coat was still in his closet. In each other's eyes they saw the knowledge of what he might have done and why. There was no denying the hopeless misery of his life on D Wing. "Let me know if he turns up," said Herbert. "In the meantime I'll be praying for him, wherever he is."

Back in his room he knelt as well as he could and said the prayer for the Oppressed, people who lived with injustice and terror as daily companions. This he followed by the prayer for Persons in Trouble and, just in case, by the Commendation at the Time of Death.

When a young guardsman delivered a vat of pea soup and a tray of sandwiches—pasta had been wistful thinking—Herbert mentioned that there might be a resident wandering outside in the dark. "Don't you worry," said the boy, who looked about fifteen. "The

Guard is on top of the situation. If he was out there we'd see him. You just relax."

Yeah, sure, thought Herbert but he wrapped up again and sent his thoughts after the man who was possibly missing and certainly lost. Perhaps an hour passed, perhaps less, when he heard a clatter of boots at his door. "Say!" said the young man, who had now become two young men, "was the guy you told me about very very old and did he live in a room with another very old guy on C Wing? Because there's a dead guy there!"

Oh no, thought Herbert, one of the entomologists! We should have got them out of here somehow, they were the frailest of us. "I'll go," he said. 'I'm a chaplain."

And which one? thought Herbert as he hurried past Silas, who seemed to be on the prowl again. "Trouble on C Wing," he explained, thinking, Homer?

Alphonse? Not that it made much difference, they were so much alike, so much a unit. How would the other manage?

In the room they lay side by side on their institutional cots, just enough space between the beds for a man to stand up. Only one of them was breathing. That was Alphonse. "Have you said goodbye?" Herbert asked gently "Shall I say a prayer for him?" He thought he saw Alphonse nod, and for the second time since sundown he commended an old colleague into the glorious company of the saints in light. He bent to pull up the sheet.

"Oh don't!" Alphonse pleaded in his wisp of a voice. "We were together fifty-three years, did you know that, fifty-three years? I don't see what to do now. No one will ever hold me again as long as I live."

As Herbert bent to hear him better, Alphonse seemed to shift and change like the beggar to whom he had once given his jacket. A great joy suffused Herbert Christmas. "I'll hold you," he said, and kicked off his loafers.

It was not long in measurable human time before Silas, spewing indignation, arrived at the door and pushed his way in.

"Herbert," he cried, "you've got to do something—" but he ended in a shriek: "HERBERT CHRISTMAS! What are you doing?" Silas feared that his eyes would wither and roll from their sockets at the sight of old Alphonse in the arms of the chaplain. Had there ever been a night so crammed with wickedness! First Lily and then Herbert! And Homer lay dead in the other cot- -no doubt he had died of horror.

The bed mate of Jesus sighed and sat up, his vision dispelled. "Piss off, Silas," he said.

GETTING TO KNOW YOU

A week after Goldengroves considered itself back to normal—restored power, decent meals—the college resumed for second semester. Much of A Wing was fairly pleased at the prospect of Chelsea's return. Sebastian, Thatcher, and Lily liked her best; they appreciated her flavor. Those three felt that, were they young themselves, they too would get something pierced. Lily fancied a diamond stud on the side of her nose; Sebastian thought that he could have pulled off a swarthy, piratical look with a gold earring; Thatcher remembered a student who'd sported tusks depending from his septum, stainless-steel tusks that could be pointed either up or down, boar or walrus, and the boy had been saving up for ivory—that was so cool that Thatcher had been jealous. But even the residents unnerved or appalled by Chelsea felt a stirring of adrenalin.

Chelsea, on her part, was still grossed out by A Wing, but she did see that all the other wings were worse. Way worse. If she did not exactly like Sebastian, Thatcher, and Lily, she felt towards them a slight mysterious inclination, which had she but known it was the call of bad-ass to bad-ass across the generations.

Nor was she as dismayed as the other girls by the latest demand of their internships: their supervisor, who admired Studs Terkel, had instructed them to make up questions and interview the residents on their own wings- backgrounds, likes and dislikes, all that happy crap—and write up something creative.

Late night in the study lounge. She and the other three sat and looked at one another. Chelsea reckoned that Ashleann might be a pain because she was the one most desperate for a good grade, but maybe terror would sharpen her up some. "So," Chelsea said at last, "what do we do about questions. What do you think we're supposed to find out." When she was with Ashleann she found her self making all her questions into statements, instinctive ballast against the chance that the other girl's chronic question marks would build up and float them all away like balloons.

"We're supposed to find who they were when they were real," Morgan suggested.

"Or who they think they were," said Kelly, who had taken a class on the vagaries of memory.

"And who they are now?" said Ashleann.

"Oh God," said the girls in chorus, "do we have to think about that?" "But they must have something in their heads?" she persisted. "Like, do they miss teaching or whatever?"

"And why haven't they shot themselves?" said Kelly in Ashleann's tone. "Yeah, we'll cover it all," said Chelsea. "How many questions will give us enough shit to write a paper, and do we all use the same ones."

"The same core questions," said Morgan, "ten, say, and then each of us add some of our own. Like, I might want to ask if they ever played an instrument. Chelsea might want to ask about the last time they got laid."

After the retching was over and Chelsea had retrieved the flipflop she'd thrown at Morgan's head, they cranked out an uninspired list. Were you ever married, did you play a sport, do you have brothers or sisters, where were you born, why did you come here to work, how do you like Goldengroves?

"Where were you when the Challenger blew up?" said Kelly, but Morgan and Chelsea said it was too recent, that the Goldengroves generation was still hung up on President Kennedy's assassination.

"Or where you were when you heard President Roosevelt died?" said Ashleann, remembering her great-grandmother.

"Goddam," said Chelsea, "they aren't that old. I don't think." "My old bug man is," said Morgan.

"Ask him about Abraham Lincoln," Kelly said.

Chelsea was all the while making herself a list of bait that might lure out something worth having. She could steal questions from those dumb emails that her high-school friends sometimes sent, ones that were supposed to make you know each other better (like four years of drugs and lust and tears wouldn't do it): If you were a crayon, what color would you be? Do you have a favorite piece of clothing, a middle name, a favorite food? Also the trick would be to follow up one question with another. Do you like your middle name? Many people did not.

Hers was Amelia (big secret), after her dad's mother, and it looked to her like the middle spot was where parents always tried to bury some worn-out sentimental crap name like it was a chewed-out dog bone. And how about "Do you have your high-school yearbook?" Would they have kept that when they cut down on stuff to move in? They would if they'd been hot, she conclud-ed. And they'd like to show her.

"What?' she said to Ashleann, surprised into a ques-tion. "What did they do in Vietnam? That's gotta be the wrong war. I had an uncle in that. But if they actually were in that one they might not want to tell. My uncle says they killed babies and cut off ears and stuff, but he's really fucked up. Who's taken a history course?"

Kelly had. She thought that it might be World War Two, if anything, and suggested further that "What mo-ment would you pick to live over?" might be a good one. So, Chelsea thought, a couple weeks to get the data, some time to let it brew, and an all-nighter to write it up. She was counting on some creative help from her boyfriend, provided they took enough breaks to fool around. Ashleann, who was afraid of writing, thought she'd like to do a group interview, so it all came together by itself. Morgan thought two or three at a time might be good, but Kelly and Chelsea thought they'd get more in privacy. Maybe more than they wanted, though.

"Alone with the old men too?" Kelly asked.

"They can't do much," Chelsea said, "except gross us out, and they've already done that." But she didn't like to think how it would be if they tried. She decided to make a point of leaving the doors open and saying it was a rule. She thought the greater hazard would be the old women, their cold knobby hands gripping her arm to make her stay; they would smell like stale clothes and show her a thousand snapshots of other people's babies. Even among the old she found men more amusing than women. One a day, she told herself, I can stand one a day. I'll take my time and go around the wing in order, unless somebody's out. I can do the couples like one person, especially Harlow and Millie. And I probably shouldn't be alone with Orin, he still seems strong. I'll do the courtyard side first and get it over with, so I'll have some practice when I get to the possibly good ones. Had she actually called any of these people even possibly good? Her mind must be turning to mush, like theirs. Oh God, already. Maybe she meant less fake. Maybe some of them would tell her real stuff.

Once again they put up notices, this time to save explanation. "Residents of A Wing," Chelsea's said, "I've got to ask you stuff about your life and write it up. I plan to start later this week. You have the right to remain silent. But I hope you won't. I can bring cookies. Chelsea Dean"

Except for Orin, who was constitutionally private, and Glenda, who had a secret, the A Wingers were more pleased than not. Most of them, after all, had made a living answering questions.

NOT A CRAYON

So here we go, Chelsea thought, with the dumb-ass questions. Full name, marital status, birthplace. How do you like Goldengroves, did you play a sport at school. Be cool. Be cool. She'd start at Glenda's end. Glenda, if she wasn't good for much, at least couldn't sneer at her if she messed it up; lucky if she could wipe her nose, much less look down it. After that, door to door up the corridor to its far end, talk to the fussy little dude with the hairless legs, Silas, cross over to the one with the beret, Sebastian, come down that side and end up with the dick flasher, Thatcher. Just as well to have some practice before Thatcher's turn, in case he got up to something.

Glenda was more pleased to see Chelsea than she would have imagined.

She had been stuck all day in a snatch of old Sunday-School song, and she wanted a hand to pull her out. Any hand would do. The song had been about a flower, she thought, though she couldn't make out why they'd have been singing about plants, given that her family had been good Baptists, not members of some vegetation cult. The words had made her cry when she was a very young child and they seemed even worse now that she felt like a very old child. *"In a dark and lonely place, many months I lay, and the world forgot my face while I was away."*

Because now she did seem to be in a dark and lonely place, and nobody ever came to see her; apparently the world had indeed forgotten her face, if it had ever noticed it. The tune wasn't pretty, but it was persistent. Glenda, humming it against her will, opened the door. And there was the pierced girl.

"I guess you've seen my notice," said Chelsea. "All us interns have to ask the residents questions about their lives and all. So is it okay if I do?"

"What's it good for?" said Glenda.

"Passing grade, if we write it up," said Chelsea.

Glenda felt herself a little amused. She couldn't remember the last time that had happened. Using me, she thought, but I'll use her too.

"Very well," she said, "but first you must sing me a few lines of something. Anything. There's a sad song stuck in my head and I need to drive it out."

Chelsea knew how that was, she'd had a dog-food commercial stuck in her head for a week once. But what in the hell was cheerful and kind of old and not too childish? She didn't want to put her first subject to sleep. Damn. "Roll me over," she sang off key, "in the clover, roll me over lay me down and do it again." She'd sung it with some older kids on a bus trip once, until the counselors made them quit, and it had stuck in her mind.

"My, my," said Glenda, "that should do it."

You owe me, old woman, Chelsea thought. I just felt like an asshole.

"Let's start with the easy ones," she said. "What's your favorite food?" "Strawberries!" Glenda said. This is easy, I can manage this, she thought. "So you were a librarian, right?" said Chelsea, who'd made inquiries.

"What did you like about it?"

"Ooh, well," said Glenda, who had liked it only moderately, "the library was nice and quiet. Clean too. It was nice to leave things in order, I think. Books. I liked books."

"Were you born in Maine?" Chelsea thought to ask.

"No, dear, I'm from New Hampshire."

"So what brought you here?" This is easy, thought Chelsea. I can do this.

Glenda turned pink. Was she blushing? "There was a young man," she said. "He was stationed at Dow. I worked at the Bangor Public Library so I could be near him."

Whoa, thought Chelsea, Glenda with a boyfriend!!! "So did you break up or what?" she said.

"He went to fight in the Pacific and didn't come back. So many young men were lost in those days! It was more than fifty years ago, but I'm afraid I have never been able to forgive the Japanese. They eat raw fish, you know, not very civilized."

Chelsea was pleased, not about the dead boyfriend but about the sushi; she had always thought of it as civilized, in fact, beyond her capacity. Glenda rolled herself over to a little writing desk and opened the drawer. "Would you like to see his picture?" she said. "I haven't showed this to anybody for a very long time."

"Yo," said Chelsea, "he was HOT! Like, Leonardo DiCaprio hot. No wonder you moved to Maine. Who's the sexy girl?"

Glenda cleared her throat modestly. Chelsea looked back and forth, peering at the faces. It could, just possibly, be Glenda, young in black and white, old in full color. "Well," she said at last, "I guess you were hot too."

Glenda warmed to the tongue piercer, who might after all be quite a good girl if she had some decent clothes and a nicer vocabulary. They moved without difficulty through questions about sports (Glenda had been a cheerleader), favorite outfit (a dark red dress she had bought with her own money after library school), siblings (none living), and the Kennedy assassination (when they'd closed the library for a day).

It was going well, Chelsea thought, and then "Have you ever collected anything?" she heard herself say. Question number fifteen. She had not yet decided, as far as she knew, whether to raise this delicate issue. She was sorry as she watched Glenda's face change, and yet she felt the buzz of the hunter who gets his prey in the cross hairs.

Glenda fought the pull of sibilants. She mustn't tell her secret, mustn't. "Sea shells, souvenir spoons," she improvised, "Scotty dogs. Oh, and, and soda bottle caps, cigarette cards, um, silver paper for the war effort, and so—and so, sometimes, so we got —SOAP, I like SOAP." There. The sensation of having vomited a toad:

huge, slippery, out at last so she could breathe. Relief and shame.

Okay! Chelsea thought. Here's my ticket to ride, here's a cookie for Beth and Millie. "Yeah, soap's good," she said aloud. "Everyone likes soap. What do you like best about it?" This was a variation on question number fourteen, "What do you love most?"

"It's so smooth," Glenda moaned, "and it's so, it smells so good, and the colors. And it's everywhere, you can pick it like strawberries. And it's MINE." She was getting worked up. Shit, thought Chelsea, she's tipped. I got to get out of here.

"If you were a crayon," she said, getting up slowly and backing away, "what color would you be?"

"But I'm NOT a crayon!" Glenda exploded. "Why do you say I'm a crayon? Not crayon, SOAP!" There were tears on her cheeks.

Man, my supervisor didn't think this through, Chelsea said to herself as she groped behind her for the doorknob. One more try. The interview had gone to hell anyway.

"What sucks worst about being old?" she asked as she backed into the corridor, but it was beyond her skill to untangle the mass of Glenda's lamentations.

TABLE TALK

Herbert Christmas and Silas Bassett had, no sur-
prise, been on one another's minds a good deal
since the ice-storm. However many times Herbert tried
not to hate Silas for having shortened his moment of
ecstatic revelation, however many times he fixed his
intention of charity on the moment of interruption, he
was confronted anew with the vision of Silas at his least
loveable, pushing and flapping, wrongheaded again.
Never mind, he would keep trying. His only progress
so far was that he could sometimes see the humor in
Silas's apparent conviction that he was having sexual
congress with poor old Alphonse, surely the worst and
least likely construction of what, even without revela-
tion, could have been an act of plausible kindness.

Silas had been not only shocked but hurt. In a world
of moral blight, he had counted on Herbert Christmas
to be his ally, had taken it for granted. Was the man not
a chaplain, mild and clean and upright? And then Her-
bert had been so unkind to him when he burst in with
the best of intentions and found— well, never mind

what he'd found, he didn't like to think about that. For the thing itself there might be some other explanation, though he doubted it, but for the rudeness no excuse. Silas, unlike Herbert, did not feel it necessary to purge himself of bad feelings. When he licked his wounds, as he often did, it was not to heal them but to savor them. Furthermore, Christmas's behavior had made it impossible to tell him about Lily's mysterious depravity, and that ate at him. It was something more complicated than simple self-abuse, though that would be bad enough. Unspeakable because unidentifiable, it offered him no vocabulary by which to reprove it.

Lily thought about Silas too, if less often. She reckoned that his credibility was not high in the Groves. She had only almost been caught in her perversion, indeed merely her preparation for perversion, and the reclamation of mind and body that she now perused would likely weigh against any incoherent tattling from a wrought-up Silas. She was using her wheelchair less often now and keeping her bed dry—those weaknesses had been the fruits of sloth. At the hour when her mind had been accustomed to begin its slide, she turned to the novels of Jane Austen and felt good sense like a cataract washing away her mental flotsam and sea drift. Now that she was paying attention to herself and not the tentacles of her dream squeeze, she was sorry to see new wrinkles. When had the underside of her arm begun to look like an ass? But she could still make out Lily Hillman in the mirror: some ghost of prettiness lingered in her face; eyes bright with mischief looked back at her. The Lily who had apparently been on some kind of weird sabbatical had come back to work.

The A-Wing dining room had tables enough to allow for visitors or permit some choice of companions. At eighty, at eighty-five, one has no time to waste on the uncongenial. Nevertheless, Silas and Herbert Christmas at last found themselves, against their wishes, at the same table; they had both been late coming in.

Lily was sitting with Sebastian, who otherwise dined by himself with a book beside his plate. He found Lily tolerable, for their conversations were brief, playful, and allusive, nothing that worked him up to a gibber. Lily felt whole when she sat with Sebastian; he had known Lily the hot ticket, Lily the scholar, and now he knew Lily the crone. All her layers came together.

"Look, Sebastian," said Lily, "Silas has got hold of

the priest and I think he means to talk about me. I believe I'd better move over there. Want to come?"

Sebastian shrugged and got up. Why not, a dust-up could be fun. He did not share Silas's penchant for chivalry, but he liked Lily better than Silas, much better. He regarded himself as fairly loyal, and if Silas meant to play the dragon, he might be moved to hoist a buckler in Lily's defense.

"You two are looking lonesome," Lily said with a smile that verged on sharkish.

"Herbert, Silas," said Sebastian, and pulled out her chair.

Thank you, thank you, Herbert thought. The Lord make his face to shine upon you and give you pie."

Silas saw Herbert's relief and hated it. And Lily, foul beyond all cleansing!

He wanted her nowhere near his food.

"I had hoped to have a private chat with Herbert," said Silas.

"No privacy at the Groves, no privacy, not at the Groves," said Sebastian and settled into his chair. Lily bumped his foot in gratitude.

"Any of you done Chelsea's interview yet?" she said.

"I thought I saw her going into Glenda's room the other day and coming out again on the run. Could Glenda have been shouting something about a crayon?"

Silas bristled. "A crayon? Of course not. She's not a child."

Lily shrugged, Sebastian lifted an eyebrow. Near enough, they implied. "She's a LADY," said Silas, "not like some!"

"Glenda has her little problems," Herbert said, "as we all do." He intended his remark to be soothing, but in this he miscalculated.

"How about YOURS?" Silas cried. There were times when the world needed so much righting that he felt exhausted at the prospect, yet his mission held: he would wrest order from chaos; he would sober the frivolous; he would burn out depravity! He would, though he were killed for it! He had no idea how close to that end he had sometimes come, or how much, even now, his table mates were longing to whack the top of his flushed and sweaty head.

Herbert was quick-scanning a mental list of things that could safely be said to the laity. To another member of the clergy, carefully chosen, he could have admitted that he had seen Jesus in the attenuating person of Alphonse the entomologist; if he chose his listener well, he would be envied perhaps, or congratulated. But it was fatal, absolutely fatal, for over-sixties to admit, in the wrong company, to any kind of vision: D Wing or its equivalent forever gaped at their feet like the Hell Mouth of medieval landscape. He might, he thought, as a clergyman, say that he was acting under his Lord's instructions, though even that remark could be perilous for the unordained.

"When you found me with Alphonse in my arms, Silas," he said, his tone firm, "I was doing God's will in the world. Our Savior says, 'Love thy neighbor as thyself.'"

Sebastian and Lily exchanged a bright glance of amusement. Bet Silas blew a gasket, thought Sebastian, but only Lily altogether understood why Silas seemed to be choking on an outrage too huge to utter. Herbert was puzzled. He could hardly have exceeded the obviousness of his reference, he thought, short of chanting John 3:16 like a fundamentalist Youth Group. He could not know that in Silas's ears the familiar instruction suddenly smacked of debauchery.

Let me help you, Silas, thought Lily. Time for a pre-emptive strike.

"I'm afraid Silas thinks that he found me loving myself when he barged into my room during the ice storm," she said, "but the room was rather dark, wasn't it, Silas?"

Sebastian grinned widely. That's my Lily, he thought, and heard the thrum of breakers, tasted salt. He remembered his back cold in the wind, his front warm against her skin. What fun, he thought, if Silas had been there to catch us making love at the sea's edge.

"Well, Silas," Herbert said, "and that's what you were rushing to tell me? You had quite a night. But why did you think it any of my business? I don't think it was any of mine, or yours either. We humans live in our bodies the best way we can; we use them to comfort ourselves and one another."

I will power-hose you from the earth like toxic mold, you dirty man, and that whore of Babylon with you, Silas's inner fiend hissed, while his better part was squeaking, Metaphor, only metaphor! How did God not see that he, Silas, was the true priest who sought to make the earth a paradise? He rose in freezing reproof and moved his plate to the table earlier vacated by Sebastian and Lily.

"Dried out like a boat bug," said Lily. "You almost have to feel sorry for him."

"Amen to that!" said Herbert Christmas, and discovered that having reproved Silas into a huff, he no longer hated him. The church has undervalued small acts of vengeance, he thought. It's wonde1ful how they soften the heart.

Adam and Eve and Pinch-Me

"So what was the matter with Glenda?" said Millie. "I hope that your interview technique doesn't involve torture?"

Chelsea was sitting at their little table with notebook, a glass of milk, and oatmeal cookies warm from Millie's oven. "I asked her," Chelsea said through a mouthful of cookie, "if she was a crayon, what color would she be. It was just to make conversation, one of those dumb questions that come in the email. Only it made her crazy."

"Goodness, she's very sensitive," said Millie. "Now I think that I would be a magenta, and Harlow would be a nice dark green, isn't that right?" Harlow nodded. "And how about you, dear? Purple perhaps?"

"Mmm, sometimes black," said Chelsea. The milk was undermining her defenses.

"Yes," said Millie, "we can see that, can't we, Harlow? But I think in the long run purple, or even red. You have a great deal of energy, you know."

"Also," Chelsea admitted, "before that, which was probably why she went nuts, I asked if she collected anything and she began to yell about soap. I hadn't exactly meant to use that question for her, at least I don't think so. It just popped out."

"Aha!" said Millie, and "Aaahgx!" said Harlow. They both laughed. "We knew about the soap, of course,"said Millie. "Everyone but Professor Bassett knows, I think, but we didn't know how she felt about it."

"Majorly freaked would cover it," said Chelsea and took another cookie.

She was astonished to find herself comfortable.

"So what else did you ask her," said Millie, "and what else would you like to ask us?"

"Last thing I asked her," Chelsea admitted, "was how she felt about being old. Not happy, I gather, but I never got any details. How is it for you guys?"

Millie grew arch. "Old? Harlow, are we old?"

Real funny, thought Chelsea. "You're here," she pointed out.

"Well, perhaps we're in early old age, what do you think, Harlow, not like the poor bug men, and one of them died. It's not all bad, you know. We're together, just the two of us, like we were at the start. Not much stress now, and we've made new friends here. Our girls call every week, and I only cook for fun now, not big meals. While the Groves isn't home, of course, it's fairly cozy."

Chelsea looked around and nodded. Not her taste, not one single thing she'd let across her doorsill, but probably it was cozy, all right. God, there was a lot of cloth, the place was all ruffles and curtains! These were serious pillow people. Photograph people too.

"Hey," she said, "wedding picture?" Lucky hit. Millie chirped and sprang up.

"Here we are," she said. "I suppose the dress looks very old-fashioned to you, but oh I did love it. My mother and grandmother sewed it for me, so Harlow and I could get married just before he enlisted and went off to Europe. The minister married us at home, at my house, and the lilacs were out and our friends all cooked things. It was a beautiful day." The young couple were not as hot as Glenda and her boyfriend,

Chelsea thought, but they had pleasant faces, they looked as though they'd have been okay to know. And although she found the style not only old-fashioned but ugly, the whole thing sounded less ridiculous that her sister's stupid wedding, which had cost a bundle and made everyone mean and weepy for weeks before it. Chelsea had sworn she'd never in the world have one of those circuses, and that had made everyone bawl and yell some more.

"So if you could live one moment of your life over, would that be it?" she asked.

"Oh yes," said Millie without hesitation, "we would, wouldn't we, Harlow? And you should know that every year at the very moment we exchanged vows we stop wherever we are and exchange rings over again." (Here she looked a little amused, as though she guessed what Chelsea was thinking: Eeew! I must not hurl, I must not hurl.) "Of course our family and friends all make fun of us and gag if they're there when it happens, we know that," she went on, "but we don't care, do we, Harlow?"

Harlow shook his head. Indeed he did not care. But he was thinking, No, the wedding was not the best moment in my life; weddings are for women; men endure them out of love. Though ours was not bad, as I recall. When Millie said "yes" and I seemed to see my life all sunshine before me, that was a better moment, I could do that one again. Sitting for the first time behind my big new Vice-Presidential desk, that was a good one too. Maybe neither one was quite as good as that winning touchdown I made in high school: I swear even the mud tasted like champagne that day. But even if I could speak, I would not say those things to Millie. Or, possibly, need to.

Millie winked at Chelsea. "Harlow won't tell you, but he'd probably rather make his famous high-school touchdown again than re-run the wedding. Men don't like them as much as we do." Harlow squeezed her hand. Marrying her had without doubt been his best piece of luck.

"Anything else you want to tell me?" Chelsea asked, when her page was full.

"Yes," said Millie, "I think you'd better let me go along when you interview Silas Bassett. If he's heard about Glenda's meltdown he could give you a hard time, and there's no reason you should have to put up with him. I could pretend to be a chaperone, he'd eat that up.

"Yo, I think I can do it myself, lady," was the first thing

Chelsea thought, as was her habit, but then, Yeah, but he's a gross old man and who the hell wants to.

"Huh," said Chelsea. "Maybe so. He was on my list for day after tomorrow, but.."

"But let's get him over with," said Millie, and rinsed out the milk glasses. "Entertain yourself until I get back, Harlow, and maybe I'll have a story."

They set off down the corridor with two cookies in a paper napkin. "I hate to waste these on Silas," said Millie, "but it will be hard, even for him, to crab at people who've brought cookies. That throws him into the obligations of a host, if you know what I mean. And I would suggest you skip the crayon question, in case he's heard about Glenda and it sets him off. Perhaps the collecting one as well. He does collect petty grievances, but you wouldn't want to hear them."

Hey, I might, Chelsea thought, but she was disarmed by Millie's air of solidarity. She could not remember a single time when the kind of woman who went in for pillows and ruffles (and marriage, come to that) had seemed to be on her side. She and Millie would not have been friends in college, she was sure of that; in fact they would have felt compelled to make fun of one another and would have found it easy work. So what was up? Did old people know how to bake drugs in their cookies? Or were there people in the world who grew broad-minded when they were old? If so, she was pretty sure she'd never met any until now. On the other hand, if she was the changed one, if it was the stuff in the cookies, maybe they'd work on old Silas Pukeylegs. And then they were at his door, which still sported its assertion that life was earnest.

"Knock, dear," said Millie, "and take the cookies."

Silas opened his door a cautious ten inches and kept his grip on the knob. They looked down at him in his wheelchair, which Millie knew annoyed him but could not be helped. "Hello, Silas," she said. "This nice young lady, whom you know, has just been visiting Harlow and me to do research for her project. I thought I'd bring her along and keep her company while she asks you some questions, and you see that she has brought you cookies, as promised on her announcement."

Silas felt a moment of fury at Millie—his moments of fury were becoming more frequent, he observed with no alarm—for her manipulation of him now, for her bad attitude in the past, for her backing up this young woman whom he knew to have upset Glenda, everyone's victim. Perhaps Millie took her part because she had upset Glenda, which would be just like her and all that heartless gang. On the other hand, he had in fact meant to let himself be interviewed, for he liked to answer questions and he liked to be the focus of attention. The cookies smelled good, and oatmeal was wholesome. "Very well, come in," he said, "and the girl can fetch another chair from the kitchen table. No, never mind, I'm already sitting down." They would of course talk in his study, which doubled as a living room.

Chelsea looked around. This was a small apartment like Glenda's, but it looked more like a real house than hers had. This old man had a ton of bookcases, books all lined up in fancy sets, no dust. His furniture, light blue, looked stiff as cardboard—a chair with a floor lamp, a little sofa thingy— and the top of his big old desk was bare. The only art was a big print of three people, whether men or women was hard to tell, wearing old Greek kind of clothes and sitting around with some pillars and trees. One of them had like a guitar, no, what was that thing called. A lute? She would bet if you pulled up their clothes they'd still have no sexes, like dolls. Fucking weird. She considered her choices when Silas told them to sit down, and sat beside Millie on the sofa, the androgynous Greeks behind her.

"So why don't I just go through these questions," she said, "and if there's one you don't want to answer, why you don't have to. Okay?"

Silas nodded. "Full name?"

"Doctor Silas Armstrong Bassett."

He said it with a roll that made the next question unnecessary, but she asked it. "Do you like your middle name?"

That was unexpected. "Yes," he said. He was not about to tell anyone how much he loved it, how as a child he thought of himself as Silas Strong-arm Bassett. How now and then, when engaged in acts of chivalry, he still thought of himself as Silas Strong-arm.

"And were you ever married?"

Silas hesitated. What version to tell? "Yes," he said, "I was married for a brief time to a young woman called Jane. We did not suit one another." And how could I put it more charitably than that, Jane, you bitch?

Chelsea and Millie both looked startled, which in turn startled Silas. Had he become so dry a stick that it was impossible to imagine him with a wife?

"So who broke it off?" said Chelsea for both of them. Millie blessed her.

Three cheers for tactless youth!

Silas flushed with anger, not at Chelsea principally, but at Jane and the embarrassment of having been abandoned. However glad you may be to see the last of an unsuitable wife, pride objects to being left. How to put it?" As you see," he said at last, "I remain here."

"Ah," said Millie, "that was before Harlow and I arrived. No babies?"

Silas inclined his head. "I think," he said, "that we will let the young lady ask the questions."

Both women, and each for several reasons, wanted to pound him in every possible tense. To have pounded him already, to be about to pound him, to be in the happy throes of pounding him. Jaws tightened.

"Brothers and sisters?" said Chelsea.

"Please speak in complete sentences," said Silas. "If you want to know whether I have siblings, the answer is yes, one of each gender, and since you will doubtless ask, I prefer the sister. What else?"

"You miserable old fart, don't give me that grammar shit," Chelsea thought. If this nice pillow person weren't watching I would rip out your nose hairs. "D'you like Goldengroves?" she said, and thought, Oh God, who could?

Silas was less red. "Why, well enough," he said. "Of course there are some less desirable elements here, as there are everywhere, but what would we do if there was nothing to improve? Yes, this place is well enough. I have all I need."

"Nice room," she said. Take that, you Sentence Nazi.

"Yes—it—is," said Silas.

"So were you in World War Two?" she asked, skipping over why he had come there to teach, which she saw by now would fetch nothing worth having.

"No, no," laughed Silas, in the chuffy tone with which the old refute the miscalculations of the young, especially about age. "I was just a boy then, still in high school, you know. I'm younger than quite a few of these old folks here."

And there's one for you, Millie.

Goddam, thought Chelsea, none of them think they're old, when anyone can see they're all near to dead. What ails them? But she said with professional civility, "Did you play any sports?" She thought it unimaginable. This one had always been a dweeb.

"No, no," chuffed Silas again, "not play, but I was the manager of the basketball team. I'm afraid it wasn't much of a team in those years. All the big boys had gone into the service, of course. Just the little young fellows left. Of course that was true of the other teams to, so we still played, when we could get enough gas."

He looked as though he expected a question. He was right Chelsea didn't understand about the gas, but she understood about him and she did not mean to subject herself to a lecture. She'd ask Millie to explain later.

"And (speaking of gas, she thought just for the record, your favorite food?

"Cocoa and popcorn," he said, thinking of Nancy, "and oatmeal cookies," he added, now that his rage was past. "In fact, oatmeal itself, with milk and brown sugar, a nourishing breakfast."

"Your favorite piece of clothing?"

"I have always since boyhood possessed a red plaid hat with wooly earflaps."

"And what did you like about being a professor?"

"I liked working with the young," Silas said. "I liked the chance to keep them safe and pure. Some of my colleagues in the department, I'm afraid, thought it amusing to shock them with filthy and subversive literature, and that had to be counteracted. Oh, I've had some fights in my day, but I always held my banner high." Silas Strong-arm, he said to himself, and smiled.

Chelsea suddenly felt that she could not bear to know what moment Silas would relive, nor did she wish to hear what story he might tell. He was the most depressing man she'd ever talked to. Oatmeal! Earflaps! Purity!

"And now before we leave," she said, covering her retreat with false civility, "do tell us about the picture behind us here." Good for me, she thought, I sounded like a fucking tea party.

"Ah," said Silas, "a favorite of mine. That's a Maxfield Parrish print that used to hang in my parents' house in Connecticut. That was how I wanted the world to look when I was a child, but I could find such peace and purity only in books. And as you might imagine, in only a few of those. I can still calm myself by looking at it."

"No kidding," said Chelsea. "And do you think those people are male or female?"

"Neither one, I think," said Silas, "that's the beauty of it. And now let me see you ladies out."

CHINESE CHECKERS

Chelsea and Silas had irritated one another in equal measure. The vacuity of her questions, Silas thought, the intrusiveness! She might have asked him for the name of his favorite poet, or his favorite essay topic, or even the hardest question on his long-ago doctoral exams. Things of importance. But no, he had been obliged to talk about oatmeal and earflaps, while that odious Millie sat by and he sheltered in his bosom a dark desire to rip out Chelsea's tongue, stud and all. Glenda, he knew, had endured from her the same questions or worse. Oh yes, he'd heard about the crayon fiasco and he'd been waiting for that query to come by; he had dreamed of crying, "I'm not a crayon, I'm a sword!" and showing the rude inquisitor what piercing was about.

The thought of Glenda aroused something visceral, a sensation familiar but ever fresh. This, he remembered, was how he felt whenever maiden and dragon appeared. On the brink of this emergent crusade, the dragons were plural, small toe-scorching creatures that danced away from his lance and nipped at his ankles. He much preferred to topple a solitary maiden-abusing colleague or administrator of either gender, preferably one of a stature sufficient to produce a good loud crash. In his dream scenario, he wiped his metaphoric sword clean, presented himself to the rescued maiden, and received for his labors appreciation, love, admiration—whatever was available. He felt, while the drama lasted, like a hero. But perhaps the transaction in retirement would be different. Perhaps an older maiden, who might fail to see or hear the waging of battle, would require emotional support of a less dramatic sort. In short, he might need to approach Glenda with no severed head in his hand.

He had often revisited the moment of ice-storm darkness when he had led the confused Glenda back to her room; he found the memory unfailingly sweet. More of that would be good. He wanted now to make her see that he was on her side, that he would protect her against all adversaries and improprieties. He wanted to offer innocent pleasure in exchange for her pain. When he himself was wheel-chair free and could drive again, he might take her to dinner somewhere outside the Groves, if she'd like it. Or perhaps she'd care to visit the local public library, where in his experience the staff was particularly helpful.

Not the college library, he thought, where her memories might or might not be happy. Not unless she asked. He himself seldom went back to the scene of his career, for he sensed that he had not been popular with his remaining colleagues, those erstwhile juniors whom he had tried to guide, and the eyes of the newer hires passed over him without pausing. Real ghosts, it is said, retain the form in which their bodies ended, but professorial ghosts go on aging and aging.

At lunch, his mind made up, he paused beside Glenda's chair and put his hand lightly on hers to gain attention. "Miss Fessette," he said in his best chivalrous tone, "may I call you Glenda?"

She stared at his hand as at some puzzling object left behind by a stranger. "How do you do," she said.

"May I sit for a moment?" said Silas, and sat. He was too moved by her nearness to be put off by her lack of interest. My poor dear woman, you have been made wary by the abuses of gossip and the intrusion of our loutish intern, Silas thought, but you can count on me,

I who mean you only good. He could offer coziness, he could offer safety.

"I wonder," he said, "whether you would care to join me in some kind of board game this afternoon. Do you have any favorites?"

"Backgammon," she murmured, but not in answer to his question. Sir John Franklin had taken backgammon boards on the Erebus and the Terror, she remembered. She did not at the moment suppose herself to be his widow, but the information lay near the surface of her memory.

"I'm not sure we have that one," Silas admitted, "but I can offer you Cribbage, or Sorry, or Parcheesi, or Chinese Checkers."

"No need to be sorry," said Glenda, finding her manners. He was offering the games of their youth. "Which do you think best?"

Silas considered. Something that didn't allow too much mental wandering, perhaps. "It feels to me like a day for Chinese Checkers," he said. He thought that the sight and touch of the marbles, and the holes into which one moved them, might keep her task before her. "You are the lady, and the guest, so you must choose your color first."

"I was always red," she said.

"And I blue." And Nancy green, and Jeremy yellow, he remembered.

Though Jeremy had seldom played a full game. It was only the right to join them that he had wanted, and they had been forced to let him in.

Silas was happy. "I have a bag of microwave popcorn," he said, "and some cocoa makings."

"I'm a nice girl," said Glenda, uneasy. Something had happened to her once over cocoa, she thought, but she no longer knew what.

"We'll have it in the lounge," Silas promised, anything to make her feel secure, though he had supposed that coziness would have been better achieved in his study, with the door open of course. And two feet on the floor, came back into his mind. That had once been the other half of the rule for visiting in some supervised residence for women—a dorm? the YWCA? The door open and at least two feet on the floor, no matter whose or in what combination, that was supposed to prevent hanky-pank. Thatcher and Sebastian could have told him of hanky-pank manageable with two feet on the floor, or even all four feet, but he and the friends of his youth, like the rule makers, had been innocents.

Glenda thought that the lounge would be suitable and they agreed to meet at three. Why they were doing any of this was not entirely clear to her, but it seemed to please the little man. She thought that he had helped her once in the dark and cold, so perhaps she owed him. It would be agreeable, in any case, to spend an afternoon out of her room. In honor of these feelings and from some dim memory of dating, she fumbled on a pair of clip earrings, discs of pearl colored plastic, and applied lipstick to the neighborhood of her mouth. At five minutes past three she wheeled herself down to the lounge. Chinese Checkers.

She had been quite good at it.

Her putative date was dithering in a way that would have made her feel attractive if she hadn't known better, if she hadn't just been looking in the mirror at the surprising old woman she'd become. Still, his solicitude for her comfort was flattering. Popcorn bowl, cocoa mugs, the board set up. Napkins, even. What would he want in return? Whatever it was, he couldn't have it, she was a nice girl.

She played with a zeal that surprised Silas and sharpened her own sensations. How long had it been since she played? She triple-jumped and crowed with pleasure. It had been nice of her mother to make them cocoa. How curious life was.

They played on and on into the early dark. Glenda won her share of games and began to feel her old self. "I'm going to be a librarian," she said to Silas.

"A useful vocation," he agreed, but wondered what had gone wrong with her tenses.

They set up another game and began it.

She peered at Silas. "Is that really you?" she said at last. "Why yes," said Silas, "I suppose it is."

"You look older," said Glenda. "So do I."

Silas cautiously admitted that they had both been younger once. "Where did you go?" Glenda wanted to know.

The conversation was becoming strange beyond his control. "I am right here, dear lady," he said and touched her hand for emphasis.

"No," said Glenda, "but you were dead, weren't you?"

This has gone too far, Silas told himself. "No indeed, Miss Fessette," he said firmly. "I am not now and have never yet been dead."

Glenda looked puzzled. "Then I owe an apology to the Japanese," she said.

"Chinese," said Silas, "these are Chinese Checkers."

"Japanese army!" Glenda said, and wept. But her pleasant delusion was over: the soldier she'd lost had never in his brief life been a nitpicker.

MANY PERVY KINDS

For a different set of reasons, Chelsea was uneasy about interviewing Herbert Christmas, but at least, she thought, he probably would not nag about grammar and he probably would keep his pants zipped, though she had heard of clergymen who couldn't be trusted on either score. But his job was kind of creepy, the whole Jesus business, shilling for a dead guy who wouldn't stay dead. Maybe yes, maybe no on that one, she did believe in God more or less, but religion didn't seem to be very good for people, it made a lot of them mean. And there were way too many pervy kinds of ministers and priests, loud tacky ones on TV and wet ones standing up to their asses in rivers, creepy nun-chasing ones and poison kool-aid ones, ones who preached hell fire and buggered altar boys. She didn't even know what she was supposed to call Herbert Christmas. She'd heard someone call him Father Christmas once, but c'mon, that had to be a joke. And would she need a whole different bunch of questions for him because of his work? She tapped at his door, which was slightly ajar.

"Come in, Chelsea," Herbert said. "I've been expecting you." Thinking that she looked a little spooked, he added, "It's not supernatural guidance. You're obviously doing one side of the corridor at a time, and I'm the only one left on this side. How's it been going?"

"You don't want to know," Chelsea said. "Millie was nice to me, though." "Dear me," said Herbert. "Come and sit in the comfortable chair, and I'll leave the door open. Did you really bring cookies or shall we use mine? And a cup of tea? Herbal?"

"Oh crap," said Chelsea, "oops, sorry, I meant to hook some from lunch but they were so awesome for once that I forgot and ate them. I guess we'd better use yours, thanks. Sure, tea would be good." She hoped tea would be good. She had never actually drunk any, but she'd drunk a great many other things and found them acceptable.

"Don't I know," said Herbert. "There are cookies that just demand to be eaten. These are packaged, I'm afraid, but first class for store cookies, chocolate chunk and macadamia nut." He rummaged down a blue plate and laid them out. The tea smelled like oranges and spice.

"Excellent," said Chelsea when she'd swallowed.

"One thing I ask people is their favorite food. Is yours these cookies?"

Favorite food! thought Herbert. Her questions won't get harder than that. Glory hallelujah! Lobster stew, Peking duck, wild strawberry shortcake, Eggs Benedict, chocolate pie with whipped cream, stuffed pork chops, Brie on a baguette, hazelnut gelato, roast beef at Simpson's, the first lettuce from the garden. He had begun to sweat. He gave thanks to his creator for branching out from manna.

Chelsea saw his discomfort and felt a tiny but gratifying shift of power. "If it was your last meal," she said helpfully.

"Ah, that's a different matter," said Herbert. "That would call for something simple and perfect. Really good bread, warm from the oven, with chilled Danish butter and just the right French wine. How about you?"

Crap, she thought, I didn't know they'd be asking me. I'd better work up some answers. "Chocolate layer cake," she said, "with lots of that dark fudge frosting. And a big glass of milk."

"Good choice! What's next?" said Herbert.

"I don't know what to call you," said Chelsea, "like your title or whatever."

"Herbert will do."

"Well," she said, and found that she couldn't quite crank out "Herbert" after all, "well, aren't you supposed to like, love everybody? Are you that kind of minister?"

Herbert was amused. "We're all that kind of minister, Chelsea," he said, "but we don't all pull it off as well as we're meant to."

"So how can you stand it here? I mean, you don't actually love all these awful old people, do you? Like, him next door?"

"It varies," he said, "some are easier to love than others, helped somewhat of course by the fact that I am now one of those awful old people myself—no, don't be embarrassed, I would have looked at us exactly the same way when I was your age. As for him next door, it's uphill work, I admit, but I'm onto it."

"But isn't he kind of awful?"

"Yes, quite. That's why it's work. Another cookie?"

"Thanks," said Chelsea. "And your regular, um, you know, people are supposed to do that too? Man, that so fucking does not work—sorry—does it?" "Not so often," Herbert admitted. "Now and then. Very pretty when it does."

"And how would you go about it," said Chelsea, "off the record." "Off the record, I found out when I was young that sometimes if I imagined very hard how the person would look if I actually did love him, it worked at least a little. Took the edge off the dislike anyway. Lately I've gone for more orthodox methods, prayer and all that. About the same success rate."

Chelsea was wondering whether Ashleann would be less irritating if she imagined loving her. Herbert was wondering whether he should dust off his old system and try that on Silas next time he was infuriating. A next time seemed inevitable.

"No kidding," said Chelsea, and finished her tea. "Well, I suppose we'd better do the list for a while. Not as interesting."

Herbert had played basketball in high school, had been the only boy of five children, had joined the Coast Guard and gone to college on the G.I. Bill. He'd come to Maine because he had a taste for the ocean and used to ski a bit too. If he were a crayon he'd be golden yellow. He'd somehow been too busy to get married, or perhaps he'd had too many sisters.

"What's your favorite piece of clothing?" "Regular or priest?"

"Regular."

"I have a blue cashmere pullover sweater that my closest niece gave me. Never thought I'd have anything as rich-kid as cashmere. It was nice and warm during the power outage too."

Chelsea decided to skip the question about what he loved most. If he said "God," she'd be embarrassed, and if he didn't, he might be embarrassed. She was once again full of cookies and saw no profit in making anyone uncomfortable.

"So what did you like about being college chaplain?" she said.

Herbert blushed a little. "I am essentially a lazy person," he said, "I like my ease, and so I found college work more congenial. I was glad to sit up all night with a student in pain or grief, if it helped; I enjoyed giving little courses in the New Testament and dealing with spiritual crises. In truth—Episcopalian of me, I suppose—! very much liked helping students to grow a little beyond fundamentalism or to deal with a load of Catholic guilt. College is often a time when those issues come up. To most of my colleagues I was fairly invisible, and I liked that too, it was restful. If I'd had my own parish I'd have had to cope with budgets and leaky roofs. And the people! I'm sorry, but churches are full of cranky people who go because they think they should and then don't like how anything is run. They get on committees and fight like tomcats. Not a clue about love. Parish priests can get pretty stressed out, I can tell you. I admired them, but I sure didn't envy them."

"But this place," said Chelsea, "isn't it nearly that bad? Do you actually like it? Is it the way you expected?"

"At least," said Herbert, 'I'm not responsible for the roof. Do I like it? I try not to think about that, I guess. The food is good. Really good, in fact. I thought it would be more private, though, lots of time to read and meditate. Instead, people think I can help everyone, they think I would LOVE to help everyone, they think I'm sad and lonely when they're not (as some of them have horribly learned to say) sharing their pain with me."

"And you say?"

"I say it's spinach."

"—and I say to hell with it!" Chelsea crowed.

"Oh, you know that, do you? How did that happen?"

"My best friend's folks had a book of New Yorker cartoons. We used to read them in case they were dirty."

They were nearly through, and Chelsea found herself almost sorry. "So," she said, "is there a moment you'd like to live over?"

There was a wariness in Herbert's answer: "To do it better, do you mean?" "I meant because it was good to begin with."

"Oh well," said Herbert, "there were some pretty intense moments on the Coast Guard boat, I felt fully alive then. And my ordination into the priesthood was rather grand." He was certainly not telling Chelsea about his visions, though he had warmed to her. He apologized in his head: You know what it really was, Lord, and I thank you for it.

"And finally, do you have any story you'd like to tell me? Anything you'd like to confess?" Chelsea thought that was quite witty of her.

"Yes," said Herbert. "Did you ever meet a resident called Donald Arnold?"

*

From Chelsea's Notebook: Get this—me drinking tea with a minister, talking all about love and shit! At the end of the interview I made a joke about does he have anything to confess, I mean it's like a cop thing to say but it's got this churchy thing about it too, and omigod he starts telling me how he thinks it's his fault some old dude on D Wing ran out into the ice storm and they never found him. How's that your fault, I said, so he says he should have traded rooms with him and saved him from some horrible old witch that used to hit him and make fun of his dick when she could catch him taking a leak, of course he didn't put it quite that way. So after I was off duty I went over to D just to sneak a look at her. Well no problem finding her, she's this giant scary blob with dyed black hair and she was bitching out a nurse. Man, I would have run into the ice storm, too. I honestly don't know how there's anybody left on D Wing. She was yelling her ass off in pretty complete sentences, though. Maybe we could hook her up with Silas.

SMOKIN'

Like Herbert, Sebastian had watched Chelsea's progress from door to door. In some measure he dreaded an interview in which he might lose control of his words. Still, if she agreed to help, he might be starting a process that would lead him back to Jane. Then again, hope was dangerous; with the pursuit of Jane, he opened himself to grief. Chelsea might refuse. Jane might be dead, or want no part of her past, even him, in which case he would have gambled his fantasy life and lost it. What would he dream about then?

While he waited, he fiddled with the surface of his study. Books lined his walls and more books sat in piles. Sebastian had preserved a rough order by period, genre, and author; appearance notwithstanding, he knew more or less where to start looking for what he wanted. He found the tumble and excess of his library not chaotic but cozy. Now, squaring the piles, he moved them closer to the walls. There, that was tidy. He teased the shoals of paper on his desk into stacks. He loved this room, his books, his leather reading chair, the rich red and blue of the oriental rug from his office, trodden bare in patches by student feet. The smell of dust and sharpened pencils soothed him, and the hospitality of worn book spines.

At Chelsea's knock he opened his door wider, made her the ghost of a bow, and gestured her to his reading chair. Was that wariness in her eyes? If so, he was flattered. She looked a bit under age, too: perhaps he ought not to offer her a drink. But Sebastian had never adapted to a university world where litigation flourished, so "Old enough for a beer?" he asked, as he had always asked his visiting students.

"Borderline," she said. "But I'm, like, at work anyway." And I think I'd better keep an eye on you, she thought. She was pleased, though. Milk had made her feel like a child, tea like a lady, so beer would have made her what, a drinking buddy? Or maybe a statistic? Did old people use roofies?

"Now," said Sebastian, taking a deep breath, "two things. I talk funny, funny, when I get into a topic. Not crazy, no, just some senile damn language glitch, damn. So. I stay silent. But I will answer the questions, your questions, yours, because I want to hire you, hire,

I have a job, if you'll do a job, good money. No, no, nothing naughty, no! Never had to pay for it! Computer thing, it's a computer thing."

"Huh," said Chelsea. "Well, you're not as weird as Harlow, all your words are okay, just kind of frequent, like, I don't know, like you got little mirrors on your tongue. You have a beer if it helps, why don't you, and we'll take the short questions first." At least he wasn't boring, she thought, or not very boring, though she wouldn't care to listen to him long.

Not as weird as Harlow, Sebastian thought, now there's a standard. Got to hand it to Harlow, though, he does get out there and takes a shot at it.

"Full name?" said Chelsea. "Sebastian George Antioch."

"George? Do you like your middle name?" Sebastian shrugged. "Dull," he said.

"Yeah," she said, "it is, kinda, compared to the other two. Ever married?"

No, and he was the youngest of three boys, and he had grown up in Virginia.

"Play a sport?" Chelsea asked, staying with the less complicated questions.

"Track," said Sebastian. "I was fast very fast. Pole vaulting too. God, I flew, flew." He was warming to the job. "Flew for the army too," he added, and saw Chelsea make another note.

"Why did you come to Maine?" she said.

"Virginia was soft, too soft," he said. "Maine had edge, colder, wilder."

Okay! they both thought. Good stuff!

"What were you doing when President Kennedy was shot?"

Sebastian's lips curved in a sly reminiscent smile. He shook his head. A lot of girls had needed comforting that night. He had fairly worn himself out.

Chelsea decided to skip the "moment you'd relive" question, in case this was it. "Well then, do you miss anything about teaching?" she said.

"Yes," he said slowly, "sharing wisdom, sharing it. One reason I post quotations. Also, irritates—" He jerked a thumb towards Silas's facing door. Chelsea grinned and pumped her fist as if to say, Yes, poke it to him. No fool this girl, thought Sebastian.

"Do you like Goldengroves?"

"It serves," said Sebastian. As a refuge, a haven, a cloister, he meant, but those were too many words.

"Favorite piece of clothing?" She'd missed that one.

Sebastian held up a finger for "wait" and went into his bedroom. Oh God, thought Chelsea, don't let it be his birthday suit, don't let it be his favorite jock strap. But when he came out he was wearing a seriously weird jacket, dark green quilted velvet with gold satin facings. "What the hell is that?" she said. "It's pretty, though."

"Haven't you ever seen a smoking jacket?" he asked, knowing she hadn't. "Well, yeah, it is kind of smokin' I guess," said Chelsea, "as jackets go. I've never seen one like that, though. What? Stop laughing at me! You mean you SMOKE in it? What for? Because it's, like, cold out, where you have to go to smoke? Do you really smoke?"

God, the chasm! Sebastian felt old for a minute. "Not now," he said. "Used to chew a pipe stem some, didn't light it much. Bad for the wind." He grasped his lapels and struck a comic pose meant to suggest Edwardian complacency.

Chelsea looked blank. Try it a word at a time, he told himself. Think haiku.

"Image:" he said. "Gentleman. Professor. Book. Pipe."

"Fireplace?" suggested Chelsea.

"Yes!" said Sebastian and high-fived her.

"And you kept it and still like it."

Sebastian nodded. "Memories of youth," he managed. And its wonderful pretentiousness, he added mentally, but didn't risk it.

"But what do you really love? Most I mean," said Chelsea.

"Words, paper, books. And once I had a friend, had. So about the job."

"Okay," said Chelsea, after Sebastian's excited oratorio had ended, "let's see if I got this. You want me to use the internet to find this old friend of yours. Yeah, that should work. If I can't I'll know someone who can. I know guys who could, like, hack into NASA. But you got a computer there, don't you want to try it yourself? I mean not NASA but like, searching."

"Not hooked up," Sebastian admitted. "I need that too—email. How—?" "No kidding!" said Chelsea. Not only old but unplugged—how was his life worth living? "College will probably give you a free account," she said, "and email's easy. Anyone can show you. But you still want me to do the looking?"

"Please," said Sebastian. "A hundred dollars for looking, expenses extra.

Another hundred if you find her."

"Whoa, serious bucks," said Chelsea. "You got it. So what's this person's name?"

"Jane Bassett," said Sebastian, looking down.

"She must have been some kind of hot," said Chelsea. Jane Bassett, she thought, why do I know that name?

"So hot," sighed Sebastian, "and so cool, and such fun."

"I was married for a brief time to a young woman called Jane," Silas said in her memory. She jumped. "Omigod! She wasn't married to that little priss-ass across the hall?"

"Yes," Sebastian said, "cruelly wasted, wasted on him. She was my best friend, Jane, best ever. Love of my life."

For a minute Chelsea nearly forgot the ick factor of old people in love. If it was left over from they were young enough to be okay, did that make it less gross? She started a clean page in her notebook. "Do you know what her real name was, not her married one?" she asked. "Because if it was me I'd sure as hell have chucked 'Bassett' right along with old Silas himself."

"Hunnewell," said Sebastian, "and I always thought of it as her real name too, so much more her than 'Bassett.'"

"And she was last heard of where?"

"San Francisco, I think. She must have gone to join the counter-culture," said Sebastian, "it's what a person would need after a dose of Silas. A dose! And that was the last I knew. If Silas knew more, which I doubt, he didn't tell me." He noticed with surprise that his speech was almost normal. I am finally doing all a person can, he thought, and it makes me peaceful.

"And, ah, about how old would she be now?" Chelsea asked. It seemed to her a delicate question like "How's her leprosy," but it had to be asked.

"In my mind," said Sebastian, "she was younger than springtime and still is. But perhaps in her early sixties now." Jane would still be young in her sixties, even seventies, he thought. "She might be involved with literature or art. Could have been teaching. Running a gallery."

"Okay!' said Chelsea. She felt professional and she liked it— a glimpse, she thought, of how some people work for a living without going nuts. "We'll watch out for west-coast Janes, maybe east coast too, probably nothing in the boring middle. Europe? Canada? Mexico?"

Oh, the world too large and Jane a jewel too small! How could he dare hope? Canada was a thought, though. Some of his students had dodged the draft in Canada and loved it. Vancouver might have been tempting after Haight Ashbury got trashy. "Yes, maybe Canada," he agreed.

Jane in Canada with geese and moose and totem poles? A country kind to the arts, though. A few world-class cities too. What he wanted now was a good stiff Scotch and some time to refit his head to this new idea. Canada, he liked it.

He stood up and thanked Chelsea, a maneuver he'd learned from one of his own much-visited professors. She rose too; it always worked. They shook hands on the deal.

"Hey," he called after her, "you didn't ask me if I was a crayon!"

"Well of course you're a crayon," she called back. "Any fool can see that. Probably red."

Damn straight, he thought, fastening the door behind her, red as a Mounty's jacket! Here's looking for you, Jane.

HUNTING AND GATHERING

The January sun was out, the temperature on its way to thirty—Thatcher consulted with himself and agreed that it was the perfect day to costume his last great flash. He had been saving that small expedition for a treat: its pleasure could be counted on, whereas the actual flashing might or might not work out well. Keats had it right; anticipation was the greater joy. Thatcher didn't read much poetry, but as a schoolboy he'd been attracted to the artifacts in Keats, the Grecian Urn, the Elgin Marbles, and had absorbed the philosophy as a bonus. It felt good to get away from his apartment, from Goldengroves. God help him, he'd begun to take afternoon naps out of sheer boredom. He had to get a grip.

His car started on the first try, a good omen. He put his hand in his pocket: he had brought the list. Good again. He sailed over the clear road, the world all blue and white around him. Perhaps he'd have lunch out, consume some decadent item not on the Goldengroves menu. The lift in his heart told him that this was one of those rare and magical days when everything works.

First the thrift shop, he thought. He'd need a hat, some beads and perhaps bracelets, and something to cover his body, some of his body, a caftan or shirt or vest—he'd keep his options open. If anyone gave him a funny look, he could say that he needed the things for a play, or perhaps that he was going to be a swami for a bazaar, it would depend on what sort of hat he found. Either a gardening hat or a turban would be excellent, both having proved effective on the Wodaabe dancers.

"Good morning," he said to the boy behind the desk. Not quite the middle-aged woman he'd expected. It was in the young man's eyes that "I'm putting on a show" would provoke a knowing grin, perhaps a rude remark. "I am giving a lecture," he said firmly, "on the Wodaabe dances of Niger, and I wish to assemble a costume. It may take some time. The dancers are males but they wear shifts and vests and beads. They also paint their faces. It is a form of display that their women find attractive." Intellectual bullying. He deplored it, but it never failed.

"That's cool, "said the boy. "Take your time. We got a bunch of vintage hippie stuff the other day and most of it's hung up." He propped his feet on a desk drawer and went back to reading *The Onion*.

Beads first, Thatcher told himself. Beads would be easiest, having lots was the principal point—colors, metals, jingle. He put a double handful on the counter and sought the hats. He hadn't even checked the prices. These days he had more discretionary money than he had any place to spend, really, and this might be the crowning prank of his life, the last outrage. No need to skimp, the Wodaabe didn't. He picked up a trashy belt of silver plates with plastic turquoise. More shine never hurt. Out of sight of the desk he spent some time trying on ladies' hats, an amusing transvestite pleasure he'd not indulged in before. Oh, it was a good day. He liked himself in a brimmed hat with a single poppy but knew that the near-turban could be a better base for an ostrich plume. Trying on the hats, in fact, had been titillating enough that he suddenly preferred a skirt to a caftan.

If he turned one back to front, he thought, the zipper could go down like a fly. So shaped skirts, butt-hugging skirts, were out. Something straight down.

And a color against which his penis would be instantly visible. He was inclining to a girl's kilt in black-watch plaid when he remembered that he intended to anoint his member with Sebastian's gift of blackberry jam. He thought that he must not let Sebastian down; they might some day become actual friends. It was not too late to make new friends, was it? In the end he chose a full white skirt, rather short, the gear of a hefty cheerleader if he read it right. Blackberry jam would stand out like a pirate's flag. He held the skirt against his waist and despite the hats he was startled by how much it excited him. There was no mistaking the sensation for intellectual joy, the damn skirt was a turn-on. Here was a small facet of himself he had not met before, and he briefly regretted the lost years when he might have gone in for recreational cross-dressing. Never mind, this new kink should ensure a display of potency that not even Chelsea could criticize. Valentine's Day, he thought, would be an amusing day for the finale flash, provided that his audience was not otherwise occupied.

Silas, at any rate, should be in. Silas amused him. He did not feel for his nitpicking colleague quite the degree of hostility that much of Goldengroves felt. That was the benefit of anthropology, he thought, if you took it to heart. If you could place the otherwise infuriating behavior of your colleagues in a broader context, you could view it with some detachment. You could say, Nit-picking, we don't mind when other species do it. You could tell yourself, Ah, they're potlatching, that's all, and then let the other persons give you the larger gifts, do the greater favors, after which you went off modestly with the loot and left them smiling. Real winning wasn't always what your testosterone rooted for, his education had taught him that. As for faculty meetings, once you saw that the small acts of aggression between colleague and colleague were like the coup counting of the Sioux, tapping other warriors to show what they could do if they were serious, why then you could play too: you could keep score of phantom wounds received and given, and it was only a game. It came to him that his jam-covered penis would be the ultimate coup stick and he bent over with silent laughter. The boy at the desk mustn't hear. Head lowered, Thatcher saw a discard pile near the dressing room, things too homemade or shabby to be kept for the shop, and oh, God did love an anthropologist! A man's black vest, embroidered in many colors by someone too high to know when to stop—it just fit him.

"Guess it will be quite a lecture," said the boy at the desk, sorting out the piles. "You can have the vest for free, we were going to throw it out."

"I think it will," said Thatcher. "Date hasn't been set yet." In case you thought of coming. "Any idea where I could find an ostrich feather?"

"Craft store down the way, maybe."

Craft store! That hadn't crossed his mind. The place was a goddam tomb treasure! He came away with not only ostrich feathers but a small mirror, jewels, glue, squeeze-bottle fabric paint, metallic trim, and other frippery he'd rediscover when he got home. He wouldn't be bored any time soon.

The black lipstick and bits of chain could wait for another day. His lunch was overdue and he was feeling his age, or supposed that might be what it was. A little woozy, a little blurred. On the way back to Goldengroves he stopped at a roadside food shack and carried off an Italian sandwich, Maine's other, non-maritime, indigenous specialty, a long and dripping feast of salami, cheese, tomato and green pepper and onion, pickles, black olives, all with a good lashing of oil. That Italian would keep him awake all night, but he didn't care.

And hadn't that once meant something else?

INSUBORDINATION

"Goddammit," said Orin, "what do we have to let her in for anyway, it's none of her goddam business what color goddam crayon I am."

"Are we going to be the only ones that won't help with her project?" said Beth.

"I could live with that," said Orin. "I talked to enough students in my time."

"I could do all the talking," said Beth, "only she'll think you're like Harlow. Anyhow, which would you rather talk to, a student or Leonie?"

"I'd rather talk to the devil than either one of them."
"A student or Silas? A student or Glenda?"

"Oh, great suffering lockjawed lobsters!" Orin said. "You win, we'll do it. But one of us surfer's hell won't like it."

Chelsea was aware at once of a mixed reception, Orin grim and silent, Beth too effusive. Man, feels like dog poop a la mode in here, she thought. Wish I was someplace else. Might as well get on with it, though. "Could I have your full names?" she said.

"I guess Orin Stanley will do," said that surly person.

"Orin hates his middle name," Beth improvised, "I never heard it till we took our vows, so I shouldn't tell you what it is either. I know how he feels. I hated mine too, it was Ivey, but I dropped it when I married so now my middle name is Fowler." She hoped that Orin appreciated the lies. His middle name was Robert and as far as she knew he liked it perfectly okay. Further, she'd invented Ivey for solidarity; it sounded like a middle name someone might hate. Her real middle name had been Ann.

Beth admitted to having brothers. Orin, cranky, disavowed his sisters. Beth revealed that they'd both been born in Maine. Chelsea, looking down her list of questions, could see none guaranteed not to offend Orin. What ailed him anyway? He'd never bothered to be rude before. He'd hardly noticed her. Born into the sharing generation, she had no concept of terseness as a value.

"What do you miss about your job?" she ventured.

"Mopping up student puke," growled Orin, "that was a winner. Oh, and cherry bombs in the toilets, big funny treat and how about messages written in shit? Do I miss it? What do you think?"

"That had to be guys," Chelsea protested, "they're nasty, girls don't write things in shit, they use lipstick. I did see a message in menstrual blood once, though. It said, 'Thanks a lot, Eve!' It had a comma, too, must have been an English major. We left it because we thought it was funny."

"It WAS funny," said Beth, "I'd have left it too. This old bear of mine hasn't cleaned dorms for twenty years, you know, but it was such a gross experience it doesn't go away. Kind of like shell shock in vets."

Orin found that he had worked off the last of his wrath on the job question and began to be sorry about putting Beth through the hoops. Chelsea was hanging tough, he gave her credit. He thought he could do factual questions now, like admitting to his middle name, though he still meant to fend off explorations of his feelings about this and that. As far as he was concerned, airing your feelings was just about in the same category as the old anthropology guy airing his dick. The men in his family had taught him by word and example that a decent fella didn't do either one.

As an apology, he admitted to having played football in high school. Beth, relieved, said that she'd played softball, in fact she'd been quite a good pitcher and the team had done well despite the lumpy old field they'd had to play on. In those days, she said, the girls were always given the lumpy old fields that weren't good enough for the boys, not that the boys were exactly playing on Wrigley Field themselves.

"That's so not fair!" Chelsea said. "I don't think it's even legal. Didn't it piss you off?"

"Sure," said Beth, "but the Suffragettes were too far back and Women's Movement was too far ahead, so nobody would have stood up for us. We would have looked like whiners."

"God, the olden days sucked," said Chelsea. Beth and Orin were startled: their schooldays, so fresh in memory, had never struck them as "olden"; olden was a word for their parents' time.

"So did you know each other then?" she went on.

"Orin and me? I went home for the weekend with my roommate from Ellsworth—I was in boarding school because I lived way out on Monhegan— and there he was. Oh my."

"So, let's see, you must have been married when President Kennedy was shot. What do you remember about it?"

"Orin?" said Beth.

Orin grinned. "When a buddy with a radio told me, I dropped a goddam mop bucket on my foot and it swole up for a week. Better'n being shot, though."

Beth said, "I was home with the babies when it came on the television.

Had all day to think about it before Orin got back. This will sound funny to you now, but I was embarrassed, I didn't think Americans acted that way anymore. Nobody thought so then. Course, we were just getting started, as it turns out."

"Now a not so important question," said Chelsea. "How about your favorite foods?"

Favorite food, that was too close to personal sappy too, but Orin pulled himself together. "Beth's chicken and biscuits ain't bad." He didn't usually say "ain't," his mother having been a schoolteacher before she married. He was talking like his uncle who had drowned ice-fishing, it was his tough-guy mask. Beth knew this and leaped in. "I have a sweet tooth, myself," she told

Chelsea, "so I'd have to say, oh, wild blueberry pie like my mother used to make. Now that has some taste, those fat old cultivated blueberries aren't worth the eating. Nothing to 'em but puff and water."

Right, thought Chelsea, who was catching on, so we'll skip favorite piece of clothing, what he loves most, what moment he'd relive. Touchy as Glenda, in his way. *Wish I'd got Beth by herself.*

"Finally," she said, "if you don't mind telling me, how do you like being at Goldengroves?"

To her surprise, Orin laughed. "I like it first-rate," he said, "I come here to watch the damn professors make fools of themselves and they haven't disappointed me yet. And when I need to, I can tell them where to head in, because we're all just folks now. Yes, it suits me right down to the ground. You're in college, though, I guess you still think they're something."

"Say what?" said Chelsea. "I think they're old and gross, is what I think. I've never seen such a bunch of freaks. I wouldn't live here if you paid me." She had in fact liked and occasionally admired a few of her own professors, functional viable professors, not old like the Goldengroves bunch. She thought it best to misunderstand Orin's opening. "You guys are younger, right?" she added. Old people all looked pretty much the same to her.

"Yes," said Beth, "we're the youngest here by quite a lot. And I don't mind Goldengroves as long as it keeps Orin amused. Want something to drink?" She'd been a bad hostess, she realized, in the preoccupation of being a good wife. She took out a half-gallon bottle of Mountain Dew and her superhero tumblers.

"So you really get off on all this?" Chelsea asked Orin. "It doesn't, like, depress you?"

"Two things I like about it," said Orin. "One is they're as crazy as they always were. Always did get a kick out of them when they weren't making me mad. Look at how they huff and fight and throw words around. Not a one of them can stand for the other guy to win, whatever the hell 'win' means to them. And they don't know a bit how to act. Not like normal folks, I mean. Two is they're funnier than hell when they come apart because they still think they're hot shits. I don't stay on A-Wing, you know, I wander around a bit, and there's guys that wouldn't give a poor old janitor the time of day that think I'm their grandpa now. Or they wrote some article about nothing sensible and thought they were king of the goddam hill, and now they can't steer their applesauce into their mouths. I tell you, I'm just waiting for the day that know-it-all Silas's bowels give out on him, that'll knock him down a notch. We'll drink a little toast to the pay-back goddess when that day comes, what do you say, Beth"

"You're so mean!" Beth said, but she and Chelsea were giggling. "Can't we drink against him now?" Chelsea pleaded. "I won't be here then, and that snotty old grammar grouch was rude to me and Millie too."

Beth raised her Mountain Dew. In the afternoon sun, Batman appeared to fly across a yellow sea. "Here's to frivolity and dirty movies," she said.

"Sentence fragments and swearing," said Chelsea, raising Catwoman. "Belching and farting," said Orin, and up went Ironman.

"Silas!" they all said, and their superheroes butted heads.

TOAD SUIT

Lily had been looking forward to Chelsea. She missed being with students: she missed the springs of energy at which a tired professor could drink undetected, she missed the sly humor, the rude slang, she missed the shifting parade of fashions and crises. Some things, of course, had been less appealing, like a whole class about to keel over from boredom. Pallid students who crept close to murmur, "I'm really sick, here's my paper." First semester finals, when the room was a chorus of maddening sniffs.

"I have some chips," she said, seating Chelsea at the table, "and apricot juice, which is surprisingly good mixed with seltzer." She remembered that students were always hungry. She had always been hungry herself, for one thing and another. "Go ahead," she said when they were settled, "ask me anything."

"For starters," Chelsea said, "how about your full name?"

"Lily Marlene Hillman," said Lily. "Well, I was christened Lily Marie, but the boys all called me Lily

Marlene during the war and I kept it. You know, after the song, Lili Marlene? 'Underneath the lamppost'? Dietrich?"

Since Chelsea obviously didn't know, Lily sang a few bars in a sultry husk. Across the corridor, Harlow stirred uneasily. Chelsea was impressed. Go, Lily! she thought. "What boys?" she said.

"Oh, soldiers, sailors," said Lily. "I used to work at the canteen and go to their dances. Lord, how the world was full of cute lonely boys in the Forties!

Here we leave the questionnaire, Chelsea said to herself, and to hell with it. This promises to be one kick-ass old broad. This'll liven up the paper. "So did you, like, ah, have sex with them?" she ventured. Lily seemed unlikely to blow up at her.

"Well not all of them," said Lily with a smile. "But I believe that I was a bit of a rascal in my day. 'War work,' we called it."

"And after the war?"

"Then I went on to grad school, which was not very welcoming to women, but I was pushy. Dull specialty, though: codfish. Not sharks, not squid, the boys took those—codfish. I got a job in Maine because they're cold-water fish. And here I am—washed up on its coast. Washed up, get it?"

Chelsea laughed, but it was really the codfish that tickled her. Dull to eat, dull to study. Poor Lily!

"So what did you do for fun, oops," she said.

"Yeah, some of that," said Lily. "Did some climbing too, skiing, sculpture course. They took the edge off my restlessness. Used to travel in the summers when I wasn't playing with my fish. Or I'd get grants to take off for Greenland or the Pacific coast, have a look at their codfish. Those were the days."

"And you never got married?"

"Thought about it once or twice," said Lily, "had some good offers. But it felt like captivity, like dancing to someone else's tune. Didn't want kids either, from what I'd seen of other people's. Now and then I took a feral cat in for the winter."

"Huh," said Chelsea, "I know what you mean. Are you ever sorry?"

"About not marrying? Depends on how it would have turned out, I guess, and nobody can tell me that. If I had a husband in good shape I might be living in a bigger cage and going out for little Sunday afternoon drives, that'd be worth something. But how many years would I have had to trade for it? What if he'd put the kibosh on travel and I'd never seen the sun come up on Luxor or drunk sludge in the Istanbul Bazaar? What would I have to remember?"

"So," said Chelsea, "are you really going to be the first person who admits that this place is the pits? Everybody else has come up with some lame reason to like it."

"Nope," said Lily, "I don't like it and I don't like my life here. A is better than C was, but that may not be so good either. I'd managed to make myself go fairly witless on C so I didn't mind so much, but now that I'm here with normal people, if you can call this lot normal, I'm back in my own head again. And so I miss things. By God I do."

I am actually feeling bad for this woman, Chelsea thought. It's like she was having a good life and some evil witch came and turned her into a toad, maybe even a toadstool. Toads at least get to hop around. Her own tone was almost kind when she said, "So what would you say you miss the most?"

"I miss my apartment," said Lily. "This isn't home.

It never will be, even if, God forbid, I live to be a hundred. For forty years I had the second floor of a big old house, and there was a screened porch that felt like a treehouse. I used to drink my coffee there every season except winter, even if it rained. Leaves all around me. My bedroom had three tall windows and in the spring the scent of lilacs came in. Oh, and stuff. I had cool stuff from all over. Rugs and tapestries and alabaster and brass, faded old Spanish saints in shrines. Stone lamps, samovars, inlaid chairs. See that painted chest under the window? Mongolian. I had the whole world around me even when I got too laid up to travel. Concrete memories. It was me, you know? It was my habitat and now I don't feel safe, not enough padding."

"Sounds too cool," said Chelsea. "And I bet you never had any little pillows with ruffles, did you?"

"God no," said Lily, "what for?"

Chelsea began to think that she had found someone whose style she might adopt, though it had all ended so badly.

"Also," said Lily, who had never had a chance before to explain what she missed, and so was, after a fashion, enjoying herself, "I miss freedom. I don't just mean get on a plane and go to Brazil, I mean get in the car with no fuss and go to the movies, buy a pumpkin, visit a friend, watch the tide come in. Room for whim and impulse. Decide what you'll eat for supper, or if you'll eat at all. Have a private life without sneaking like a teenager. Sorry, was that rude?"

"Nah," said Chelsea, "I was out my window all the time when I lived home."

"Well I wish I could get out mine," said Lily, "just for the hell of it. But what would I do then, sit around on a snow bank till I froze? No wonder this is called the winter of our lives. Those Eskimos are more honest when they put their old folks on ice floes. Here we just get stacked on ice so we won't smell dead."

"Eew," said Chelsea, "and I notice it doesn't always work. I could name a few people who smell brain-dead anyway. So what else? Get it on out, I'm already bummed."

"Last one," said Lily. "I miss my body, my real body, where my skin was smooth and white and nothing slid south. No brown spots, no ridges on my nails, no volunteer chin hairs. It had a lot of energy, that body, it could party all night. Hell, it could high dive and sky dive and it could have dumpster dived if it had to. Tight waist, nice ass—I have a good deal of independent testimony on that score—and have you ever heard the expression 'sweater girl'? Never mind, I can see that you haven't. I'll show you."

Lily pulled a photo album from her bookcase.

"You don't have as many books as Sebastian and Silas," Chelsea observed. "They're lit guys," said Lily, turning pages, "and love many things. Plus English profs have a way of hanging onto stuff that somebody might think they should have, even if they never look at it themselves. Classics, y'know? Well of course I've got *The Faerie Queene*, what do you think I am? they say. Believe me, I've known some of them well. Me, I mostly get library books and give them back when I'm done. I don't feel the need to take out adoption papers just because I've read a thing once. So here, take a look at the real me—here I am in my war-work days in Chicago and here I am on Schoodic Point in a bathing suit when I first joined the faculty. Not much difference. But NOW! Who the hell zipped me into the toad suit? Okay, I'm done. Any other questions?"

Chelsea was staring. She'd thought Glenda was hot

in her youth, but now she saw that Glenda had been more like slightly warm, kind of pretty, good enough for the hot boyfriend, but Lily! Yowza! And she'd been a professor? Of codfish? She could have made big bucks in Vegas. Lily preened inwardly at Chelsea's dropped jaw. She liked this metal-studded intern quite a lot, she decided.

"Yeah," said Chelsea, "I've got a question. Did you sleep with any of the guys on A Wing? I mean, you don't have to answer that, but they must have been after you. I'm just trying to get my head straight."

"If I had, which one would you guess?"

Chelsea thought. Absolutely not Silas. Probably not Harlow or Orin.

Probably not the priest. "I'd say either Thatcher or Sebastian," she said. "Yes," said Lily, "it was one of those." Her tone was warm but final.

Chelsea remembered that she had too little privacy and decided not to push. "Thanks," she said, "this was actually fun: apricot and seltzer are a good mix, and you've got the best stuff I've ever seen, I mean the room stuff. Now I want to have a house like yours some day."

"I think it would suit you," said Lily, and rummaged

in a basket. "Start with this," she said, and handed Chelsea a strange object made of woolen strips and tassels. There were beads too. "If you've got a camel's head dress, it's way too late to go for ruffles," she said. "Don't know why I brought it, got no place to hang it. I just panicked and grabbed stuff when I packed to come here."

Chelsea, pressing the scratchy head dress to her chest, beat her tongue bolt against her teeth so she wouldn't cry. "Thanks," she said. "Stay cool, Lily. Cool not iced." She wondered whether she and her boyfriend should sometime spring Lily for a night's bar-hopping, no toad allusion intended.

FOLKWAYS

Expecting Chelsea, Thatcher carried his half-finished costume to the bedroom. "Why are you sticking a feather on a turban" was probably not on her questionnaire, but she looked like a girl who could improvise. He didn't mind talking to her, though all he really wanted was to go on with his project, which both rejoiced and consumed him.

Preparing for Thatcher, Chelsea hooked a napkin-full of cookies from lunch. This was her last chance to make good on her flyer's suggestion that she could bring some. Also, she thought the men were less likely to serve refreshments, not counting Herbert, who, being a priest, was to her mind not altogether a man anyway. Furthermore, people who were sharing food gave more open interviews, she thought. Was that because of the food, or did the same people just share more easily, food and information both? Or was there no connection? It was as scholarly a question as she had ever had occasion to ask herself.

When Thatcher opened the door, Chelsea's eyes

sought his fly. All safe, she thought. "I have brought peanut-butter cookies for the interview," she said.

"Great," said Thatcher, who had not missed her inspection. "I've got some orange juice. Good old peanut butter, American's comfort food! Do you know, I don't think I've ever seen a culture that didn't have some kind of mushy feel-good food—Hawaiian poi, Buckovanian nachynka, is this a human need? And if so, exclusively human? Carnivorous pets will lap up baby food if you offer it, but they aren't programmed to hunt it. No sport anyway, in a thing that can't run away. Or do some animal innards seem like mushy feel-good treats?"

Gross! thought Chelsea. I've hardly sat down yet and he's talking about, like, rat guts. "So it sounds like you traveled a lot," she said. "Did you buy a ton of cool stuff like Lily next door?" She looked around his room. There were some masks and worn figurines, but no glitter.

"Not so much," said Thatcher. "Too often I'd have had to hump it out on my back, the places I was. Most of the stuff you see was given me by one headman or another. No, I ate strange food and made strange friends and learned surprising things, but I traveled light. It's an exciting discipline, Anthropology. Do I know your major?"

"Special Ed," said Chelsea, and despite the almost guaranteed chaos inherent in her choice, all at once it sounded dull. She could see that Thatcher thought so too.

He paused with the orange-juice carton in his hand. "Huh," he said. "There are one hell of a lot of you guys. Tell me, are there so many messed-up kids that we need this tsunami of teachers for them, or are we training so many Special Ed teachers that the docs are diagnosing to keep up with them? What do you think? Who drives the market, buyers or sellers?"

She had rarely been asked to hypothesize about anything, let alone something so tricky. Her classes were large, her major undemanding. She bought time with a mouthful of cookie. "I think," she said at last, "that the doctors do it for themselves, so they control both buyers and sellers." She didn't know whether she thought that or not, but she'd said to herself, Take a shot, Chelsea, take a shot!

"Not bad," said Thatcher and, having poured the juice, put the carton away.

"Now about this interview," she began, wondering how she had lost the upper hand so soon.

"Of course," said Thatcher. "Your turn." He bit a cookie.

His full name was Thatcher Stuart Sinclair, to which he did not object. He'd been born in Fall River, Massachusetts, and although he'd been married once, he was amicably divorced. "She was right," he said, "I was never home when I could be in the field. We loved each another in a laid-back kind of way, but one day she said to me, 'Thatcher, it's not enough to keep me going,' and I didn't argue. I missed her for a while but I was never too lonely. I'm not a team player by nature. Oh, though I did play lacrosse in boarding school, since I hear that's one of your questions."

Chelsea was writing as fast as she could. "Okay," she said, "what did you do during the war?"

"That was my boarding-school period," said Thatcher. "As I recall, I mostly tried to get enough to eat. Nothing's as hungry as a school full of teenage boys, and rationing was on. Amazing now to think of the stuff it was hard to get—sugar, bananas, butter. We scrounged from people's fields and orchards but we got expelled if we were caught. Ever since, if I'm working in strange parts and I'm offered something really odd to eat—and the locals will sometimes test your manners with stuff they wouldn't touch themselves, by the way—I call back the Thatcher who would have eaten anything that couldn't outrun him."

"Odd like sushi do you mean?" "No, odd like fried elephant dung."

"Have another cookie!" said Chelsea. "Do you remember when Kennedy was shot?"

"Sure," said Thatcher. "I was on sabbatical checking out Papua New Guinea on my way to Australia; got an itch to see the tree-kangaroos and the giant butterflies. First day there, so I was still in a hotel. And this waiter runs in all wide-eyed and yells something in Pidgin. I don't know Pidgin, but it's one of those languages like Norwegian that now and then sounds almost familiar for a minute. I don't remember what he said exactly, I'm making this up, but it was like 'Bigfella Kennedy buggerupim bangbang!' I could tell it wasn't good. So I ran outside for a newspaper and everyone on the street was crying. Quite moving. They gave me dinner free that day because I was an American, it was a sympathy gesture. Good dinner too—pork and sweet potatoes and rice and greens all mixed up together, I remember it well."

Goddam, thought Chelsea, this man's world is bigger than Jupiter and twice as weird. "But you're shitting me about tree-kangaroos, right?" she said.

"Nope, you ought to see those little buggers jump. There are Birds of Paradise there too and, despite what the poets thought they really do have feet."

"So why are you at Goldengroves after all that," she said, "and how can you stand it?"

"I thought it would be easy," he said, "but I hate it. I figured no house and lawn to bother with, dinner cooked, people I know to chat with when I've got nothing better to do. Joke is that since I've retired it's like I don't ever have anything better to do. No classes to prep, no students to see, no lame-ass papers to grade, no meetings to stir up. I've fallen out of the loop for fieldwork. I could travel, just travel, but I've lost my edge. This damn place sucks all the juice out of you."

"No doubt," said Chelsea. "So is that why you, you know, flash people? To have something to do?"

"YES!" cried Thatcher, "but in this place, even that's kind of boring."

Chelsea thought that it would be kind of boring any place, she didn't get it at all. Not to say that she'd never mooned anybody when she was out with a gang, but that was a quick, jubilant gesture of rudeness and then it was over. She didn't walk around with the seat of her pants down waiting to see if somebody would notice she had an ass. No surprise factor there, and if you're, like, a guy, people probably can guess that you have a dick. Not like you collect, say, model trains and want to show everybody your new coal car.

"So are you hoping for some kind of result?" she said. "And we're way off the questionnaire again."

"I want someone to yell or throw a bucket of water on me, I don't care," said Thatcher. "I want to be NOTICED, so I know for sure I'm not dead. Oh hell, I suppose I'm like a kid who's bad so he'll be whipped instead of ignored. That's a humiliating thought. Thanks for asking, Cookie Girl."

"But you still intend to do it? I mean, you can keep your pants zipped and I'll throw a pan of water on you right now if you want. We're supposed to, you know, help the residents."

"Oh, shut up," said Thatcher. "Yes, I've got one more

flash in me and it's going to be a doozy, you just watch for it. This would make the papers if I took it to the streets, but I'm going to break this fish-faced gang on A-Wing."

"Right on," said Chelsea. "Now back to the stupid list for a minute, what's your favorite food?"

"That's dull. It's whatever I haven't had for a long time, I guess. The other day I had an Italian sandwich that was near heaven."

"Favorite piece of clothing?"

"God, Chelsea, who made this list? Do I look gay to you or what?" He was definitely not telling her about the white cheerleader skirt after that crack, though. "Okay," he said, "I've got an old safari jacket that's been all over the world with me. It's got blood and berry stains from five continents, I guess, though yes, I have washed it from time to time."

Five? thought Chelsea, naming them in her head. "In that case, a last question. Is there a favorite moment you'd live over? You got a story about it?"

"No," said Thatcher. "For me it's the next adventure that's the best one, or it always has been. May have to rethink that though. I like the story that hasn't been told yet. Unheard melodies are sweeter, you know?"

*

From Chelsea's notebook: Well that was different. Old Thatcher must have been a pistol in the classroom. He makes you think every fucking minute, no let up. Why are there so many Special Ed kids, what's pijin, what's rationing, what's the fun in flashing? I don't know whether to be glad I'm not an Anthro major if all the profs are like that or sorry that Special Ed doesn't kick my ass that way. I said to my boyfriend "What's pijin?" "Pijins in the grass alas," he answered, "I have a Gertrude Stein paper." Ha ha, very funny. If I change majors it won't be to English. But I'd like to know weird stuff like Thatcher and buy wild stuff like Lily. Oh fuck a fucking duck, am I going to have to change majors and be in school forever?

SILAS GOES DOWN

Thatcher had set his alarm, but anticipation waked him first. It was the day, it was the day! He planned to be waiting for the others at lunch, posed and smiling by the dining-room door, too flamboyant to miss. And then for his swan song. No, his swan dong! Euphoric, he laughed aloud at his own joke. Yes, he would steal down the hall and take his place just before the others emerged from their rooms. As he sipped his coffee, he imagined their reactions. Sebastian and Lily would smile, he thought, and Lily might give him the gift of a bonus shriek. Herbert, Herbert would forgive him. For something spectacular in the way of outrage, he'd have to count on the others, the wives and Glenda, the husbands and Silas.

He reviewed the order of his dressing. First the skirt back to front, zipper down; then the belt. Then the vest. Then the necklaces. He had rigged a mirror to hang below his waist: all the Wodaabe wore such mirrors, fancy ones if they could afford it. Thatcher had tricked his up with fake gems glue-gunned around the edge. He would wear his tennis shoes with the outfit, he thought, and he would dress early, which should give him time to get turned on by the skirt and make the jam worthwhile. He would start the last hour by painting his face, allowing time for corrections. And then he would tuck a plastic lobster bib around his zipper area to protect against stain, rub on the jam, wash his hands, pull on his plumed turban, and step out into the hall. He could hardly wait.

Silas had waked up cross. He thought that he had once liked mornings best. He did not like this one. In his spells of sleeplessness he was beset by old grievances and sometimes carried them back with him into his dreams.

Apparently he had done it again, for he awoke full of outrage not only at a laughing Jane but at a hopelessly frivolous colleague who twenty years earlier had written his request for promotion to Full Professor in mock-heroic couplets and, worse, had gotten it. Had in fact gotten it several years before Silas with his flawlessly sober presentation had managed to catch up. Silas was baffled anew that the world worked so badly. Also, this was the last day of the wheelchair, to which he had become rather attached. True, he was taller without it, but he was slower too. No more swooping down; he would be back to creeping up. What's more, it was Valentine's Day, which always irked him. God, the drugstore racks of unfettered emotion and tasteless insinuation! He had to avert his eyes. He could understand something discreet for courting couples—he had in fact considered some small token for Glenda and then thought better of it—but cards for mother father daughter son friend teacher godchild neighbor brother sister mailman dog! The world was gummy with sentiment. He needed a poached egg and some rye toast.

Eleven o'clock. Thatcher applied a constellation of blue dots to his cheekbones, which he had lightly yellowed with cornmeal. Oh, it was good! He colored his lips black and smiled at himself for some time. Afterwards he fastened the lobster bib around his ersatz fly and spooned blackberry jam into the palm of his hand. The seeds, he knew from a trial run, would make him itch a little, and the jam would not hold forever, but never mind, the effect was all he could wish. The deep purple glaze of his penis glittered in the morning sun. As for the bib, it looked so silly that he left it on for its irritation value. Settling his headgear, he stepped into the corridor, his heart bouncing. When had he been so intensely alive? When had life last been this amusing?

Silas proposed to go to lunch early. His egg had been under-poached, about as appetizing as a misplaced sneeze. He wanted lunch asap and he wanted his favorite table and he wanted what he wanted, dammit. He still felt cranky and ill used. When would the world shape up and grow sober? Trouble and stress, he fussed to himself, trouble and stress. He rolled his wheelchair across his threshold and glanced left and right, as he had done all his provident life. Left! His head swiveled back. What monstrosity was that? He turned his chair for a fuller look: Thatcher, but what was he playing at? Women's clothes, by all that was holy, with a wad of necklaces and a foolish hat! What was that on his face? Why was his lobster bib hung like an apron? Was that his PENIS? A great howl of rage rose up through Silas from groin to tonsils, fury and outrage at the world's frivolity.

"BE SERIOUS!" he screamed and launched himself down the hall. "BE SERIOUS!" and all the jokesters and buffoons, the clowns and mountebanks of his life seemed to pass in abominable review—his brother, his wife, his colleagues and classmates, a crowd beyond counting. He whipped his wheels till they hissed as he flew down the carpet. A Wing rushed to look out its doors. "BE SERIOUS!" He was outraged at the insult to hats and penises and lobster bibs and cheerleaders, things that had their proper and sober uses. "BE SERIOUS !" he howled and in the mirror that hung at Thatcher's belt he saw up close his own world-swallowing mouth.

Thatcher too had been open-mouthed as the missile that was Silas launched itself. He had time to appreciate the magnificence of his colleague's outrage and to be happy that so many people were watching. After that there was some pain.

"Gluurg," said Silas, tasting blackberry. His overloaded mind went white, he pulled back gagging. His mouth empty again, he laughed from shock, and having begun, he laughed on from sheer bitterness. He had been wrong, wrong, and his life wasted: the world, he saw now, could not be made serious. Its answer to him had been a mouthful of Thatcher's jam-covered penis: Fuck you, Silas, with knobs on.

He saw that all of A Wing had observed his rout, their mouths ajar as well.

You might want to close those, he thought grimly. But no, not quite everyone. Glenda, caught up in her own innocent head, must have had disregarded the shouts. He could yet sift something from the ruins of his inner life. In a world that refused reason, order, and decency, there was still Chivalry. He still had that.

In the morning he and Glenda were gone, taking along (it must be supposed) enough soap to supply even the most antiseptic honeymoon.

*

From Chelsea's notebook: Omigod omigod it was worth this gnarly job just to see it! So here's Thatcher dressed up in a wild outfit with his face painted and it's the big flash he told me about and he's got something dark and sticky all over his dick. And here's old Silas yelling and screaming, so we've all run to see what's up, and Silas is, like, zooming down the hall in his wheel-chair like it's the Special Olympics at Daytona, and then SMACK they're all tangled up together. And I'm dying because he's got jam on his face and I'm sure he had Thatcher's dick in his mouth, oh please god let it be true. Let it be true and I'll give up drugs for a month, I swear, because who needs them anyway if life gets like this! Then Silas backs up and begins to laugh and it's a bad laugh, you can feel it even if you've never heard him laugh normal, which most of us haven't, and Thatcher is still kind of sitting on the floor in his funny clothes looking surprised. Orin and Harlow are the nearest, so they go to help him up plus I bet they didn't want their wives to get any ideas about games with jam. Thatcher stands up like he hurts, I guess he probably got bitten some, but he looks happy too. "That, Gentlemen, is called making an impression," he says as they help him through his door, and I like knowing what he means. Then pretty soon Sebastian takes a plate of lunch and a bottle of whiskey and heads down towards Thatcher's apartment. So I say to him, just to say something, "Should somebody take one to Silas?" and he says, "Don't you think he's eaten enough for a while, eaten?" and he winks and we both snort. He knew Herbert was taking Silas a plate, tho.

These guys are not laughing as much as you'd expect, they just seem kind of peaceful. Behind their smiles I have a feeling they may be, like, sorry for Silas, I don't get it. Me personally, I'm laughing my ass off. P.S. Thatcher still has leg hair.

SEBASTIAN ASCENDANT

In the week after Silas and Glenda's elopement, A Wing talked of little else. So rash! So unexpected! Did Glenda take along the soap? Did Silas know by now that they had been right? Did he indeed love her or was he so intent on saving face that he would have eloped with a fence post? "If we'd known ahead of time we could have had a shower for Glenda," said Millie, and meant it, but first Beth and then all four of them thought Shower—soap! and laughed until Harlow choked. "Guess Silas could have used one too," said Orin, and they were off again. For Orin, the whole thing was better than Christmas—two professors wrapped up in foolery and tied with a bow. Nobody had much to say about Thatcher, though Orin did remark, "Damn fool deserved to get bit." Thatcher knew that Silas had stolen his spotlight, but he was not as much put out as he would have expected. He had at last made something happen, and that was all he needed. His last flash, in its strange outcome, had altered the lives of two people, at least two people, evidence that he was not dead yet.

In the second week, word passed from management to Herbert Christmas to A Wing that Silas and Glenda had applied for the three-room on C Wing still occupied by the bereaved Alphonse, who would probably then move back to one of their apartments on A. This news was regarded as not only interesting but good. Silas out of their figurative hair was a benefit, but Silas out of their lives, they were beginning to understand, would be a loss. To those in danger of terminal lethargy, a good reliable irritant has its value.

Sebastian himself was of several minds about Silas. He had mildly disliked him even before they retired, but Silas just across the corridor, a Silas without the diversion of committees and college politics, had been far worse.

Nevertheless he was impressed by his old colleague's rise from what seemed likely to have been the worst moment of his life. He would have bet that Silas was too mired in his own rut to change, and he would have lost that bet. Instead, that erstwhile prissy old fart had laughed the bitter laugh of enlightenment and galloped off with a woman thrown over his pommel. Not much of a woman, but still! For the first time in four decades Sebastian almost liked the guy.

Further, with Silas gone from A Wing, his own hunt for Jane felt less covert. He refused even to think "more legitimate," Jane was a free agent, as was he, and yet there was something—a breach of some primitive code? It was the sort of thing Thatcher might know. In any case, with Silas no longer before his eyes, he could relish his own suspense, his giddy swing between hope and fear. He wondered every morning whether Chelsea would bring news of Jane that day, and he kept on hand enough cash for payments and bonuses and jubilation. He had set up an email account at the college and knew in theory how it worked, but he had sent no messages yet. He wanted his first email to go to Jane. He had been modern with her once upon a time, and he would now, God willing, be modern with her again.

Three weeks after their interview, Chelsea approached Sebastian in a way that he would have described as a sidle in anyone else. Grinning, she waggled her fingers in a "Gimme."

"A hundred bucks for the work, another hundred for finding her, am I right?" she said. "Fork over, dude."

Anybody, not just Sebastian, might have spoken in circles at such a moment. Sebastian's circles fell apart into little curves. "Have you? Jane? Are you? Really? Jane? How do you? When? Jane? Is she? Where?" He stopped when Chelsea began to laugh at him.

"Yeah, stay cool, we got her. I'm sure of it. Jane Hunnewell, formerly Bassett, age 62, lives in Toronto. Works in the Victoria College library at U. of T. We checked her photo on the college web page. Not bad for her age, I gotta say. Her email's jane.hunnewell@utoronto.ca."

Sebastian wondered briefly whether he was having a stroke. His innards trembled and twittered, his heart clenched, his head buzzed. No, no, he mustn't die now, not on the edge of fulfillment! "Write it down," he croaked. He couldn't stop his hands shaking. He had meant to offer Chelsea an extra fifty to make the first contact with Jane but, shamed by the intrepidity of Silas, he gave her the money as a bonus for having been the one to think of Canada. "Indebted forever, forever," he said to her.

"Cool," said Chelsea, and he thought that she looked happy for him, not just for the money. "Lemme know how it works out," she said.

Sebastian had a very stiff scotch straight up, which he reckoned would either calm his nerves or finish him off. He drank it pacing the carpet, casting propitiating looks at his computer. What tone should he take? Tentative, passionate, jocular? He resolved at last to sound as much like possible like the old Sebastian, by which, paradoxically, he meant the young Sebastian.

Sebastian of the early 1970's, laid back but full of warmth. He wrote twelve drafts in pencil on lined paper, the last five of which were more or less legible.

He typed in Jane's address and gazed at it. He had not understood that technology could be so fraught with emotion. For the subject line, perhaps, an allusion to one of the poets they'd read together? "Raise me a dais of silk and down!" he wrote. If she still knew her Rossetti, she'd hear the conclusion: "Because my love is come to me." And yet it sounded amused, like "Well, I'll be dipped in down!" He topped off his drink. His hands, on the keyboard, had never looked so old. "Yo, Jane," he wrote at last. "Sebastian here. Remember me? That spectacularly hot dude with his feet beside yours on the porch rail? Your drinking buddy left behind in your sudden but doubtless wise escape from Maine and him who shall remain nameless? At the risk of sounding soppy, I have actually never stopped missing you.

On impulse I asked a tecky student to find your email for me—apologies if that was stalking, of which we once knew nothing—and I must say that emailing you so restores my youth that I may break out in bad sonnets any minute. But enough, unless—or until?—I hear from you that you'd find it fun to be in touch." Bullseye, he thought. And the closing? "Love" might be pushing it. He settled on the somewhat antiquated phrase "As ever," which seemed to him to say a number of thing, all of which Jane, the Jane he had known, would be able to read.

For five days he checked his mail in ever increasing panic—was he doing it wrong?—but on the sixth he saw her name. His throat closed. The subject line was blank—oh god, the suspense of it! But when he opened the message, there was Jane's remembered voice: "Sebastian, you old goat, stalk me as much as you like! You were the only thing I regretted leaving, lobster rolls aside. When I began to figure out how much I regretted it, the time for casual calls or notes seemed long past. And so I drifted until I had drifted clean out of sight. No tool to measure for how high I am from your note! Do you still read Rossetti or was that a resurrection special? I tried marriage one more time and it was better than Silas but not good enough to justify the ironing. Divorced now. No kids. Got a couple of ferrets, though, Greer and Cameron, and of all things a library degree. Lots of peace in Special Collections. Tell me your tale, Ancient Mariner. Toronto isn't so far from Maine that we might not worry down another bottle of wine while we can still get our feet up. What do you think? Cheers, Jane."

I think, Sebastian answered in his head, that my heart is full of wings. I feel like I've swallowed a gull, no, a flock of gulls. I think that you are still you and I am still I, and even if we never add up to us, the satisfaction of talking to you through the air is milk and honey to my soul. And now that I feel renewed, I think that if Silas is strong enough to learn, then I am strong enough to teach. I shall take this damned oratorio- speech, if it persists, out among the others, the nurses and visitors and interns, and let them learn what can happen even to a mind that loves words. They may as well see it coming.

It was the time of day when much of A Wing gathered in the lounge like people who remembered cocktail hours. Nowadays they chatted, Sebastian supposed, or perhaps watched the news. Here he came and they could stare if they wanted to. Beaming, striding four inches off the floor, he entered and sat down next to Harlow. "Not as bad as Harlow," Chelsea had said. But Harlow must be seen, in some measure, as his brother in Babel.

Harlow smiled at him. "Good," he said cordially.

"Good" thought Sebastian, "he's saying 'good,'" I think, but does he mean "good to see you" or "good afternoon" or "dinner promises to be good"? Sebastian, like Millie, was allowed to make of it what he could.

"Yeah," he said, "we were good at what we did, Harlow, weren't we, what we did? We were good."

CHELSEA CONCLUDES

From Chelsea's Paper: So there's my interviews, but being that this is for credit you probably want to know what I really learned, besides all that about old-time wars and weddings, I mean. So here it is, this is what I learned, and it's not good news. When I started at Goldengroves I thought they were all really horrible, like Stephen King horrible. They were ugly and they talked funny and they peed and choked, or some of them did. My family is so dysfunctional that I never even met any old relatives, so you can imagine. It was like these people were total aliens from a really really distant star. After a while I thought maybe they were aliens who had taken over the bodies of regular people at some point, because now and then you would see just a second or so of a human person in there. But on the interviews I found out for sure that they are people like us only this thing that happened isn't extra-terrestrial, it's just time. And it will get all of us if we aren't lucky enough to die first. Some of them think they're still young, they're young inside, and that totally freaks me out, because how do they feel when they look in the mirror. They know things they can't use. They had stuff they couldn't keep. They still love, sometimes dead people or far away people, sometimes even each other. Two of them actually eloped!!! (Though one of those is pretty much gone in the head, the soap stealer I mentioned, and the other is very strange in his own way, trust me.) Some of them tell me they're happy, and I don't know which is worse, (1) they actually want so little that it's true, or (2) they are so miserable that they have to lie. In conclusion they are like those bi valve things—mollusks, right?—all weedy and rough on the outside but inside all naked and helpless. They are still in there, it's too horrible, much worse than Stephen King. I did not want to know any of this, no no no, thinking of it will make me feel worse all my life until it gets me too, and in conclusion again I do not see any comfort for this in my current major, Special Education, so I am switching out. My boyfriend says try English, but I am still thinking maybe Anthropology so I can see how people in other cultures deal. I hear the Eskimos have some good ideas. The End.

EPILOGUE

The Silas who returned to Goldengroves with his slightly demented bride was a wiser and more humble man, and thus enjoyed a cordiality from his peers to which he was unaccustomed. They had discovered that they could endure his opinions in the abstract; what had riled them had been his monumental bad manners in pressing them. He had been arrogant. Now he was not, very. The discovery that Glenda was indeed the soap thief had added a dimension to his humility: he was not, it seemed, always right. As Glenda declined, he found that it was necessary to rescue her every day, which suited his temperament. He had needed to love someone steadily, not episodically (a maiden here, a maiden there). There was not a great deal of sex, not to say that Glenda didn't like it, but her shifting view of who Silas was—sometimes her lost soldier, sometimes Sir John Franklin, perhaps others as well—made him feel that he was taking advantage. By nature more chivalrous than amorous, he was content. As for Glenda, whoever that man was, he made her feel safe for the first time in years. It was no longer necessary to hoard anything. They gave four suitcases of soap to a shelter for the homeless.

Sebastian and Jane met in Toronto for a heady weekend that ended in bed.

In the euphoria of rediscovering one another they believed for a year or more that they were in love, but in the end each decided that it was not the case. They were close enough to admit it to one another without rancor, after which they got together at least once a year and emailed nearly every day. They were indispensable flirtatious best friends. Sebastian was content to have lost his nocturnal dreams of Jane, dreams that after all had sometimes ended in weeping, in exchange for a friendship so joyous. They wondered sometimes what they would do if they became too decrepit to travel—should Sebastian move to Toronto and get on the Canadian health plan? Would marriage be required for that? Whatever they had to do, they agreed never to lose their connection again.

Thatcher's strange adventure with blackberry jam and face paint renewed his vigor. He got in touch with old friends and revived his connections in the world of anthropology. Many an expedition, as it turned out was glad to have along a man of such wide experience and good humor. The college, too, noticed him again and gave him an adjunct course in Comparative Culture. He taught every £alt when the academic lust was upon him, and went on scholarly adventures as chance permitted in the other seasons, keeping Goldengroves as his base and resting place. He disappeared in the neighborhood of the Victoria Falls on his 78th birthday. He would have liked that.

Orin died of a heart attack in his mid-sixties. He and Beth had always known that this might happen, and thus he escaped the decay of later age that he had dreaded. Beth, as his widow, was qualified to stay on in a smaller apartment. At first she made long visits to their children, but after some time she realized that she preferred hanging out at the Groves with Millie, though they missed Orin when the three of them got together. Harlow and Sebastian were friendly, but it wasn't the same. Beth and Millie quietly agreed that if Harlow, who seemed frail, was the next of them to go, they might save money by getting a three-room apartment together. "Like a girls' dorm," said Millie, and Beth remembered the silly fun of her boarding school days.

Lily lived long enough to enjoy the revelation of the real sex life of the Giant Squid. As it turned out creature was as big as a school bus and twice as clumsy. In 2005, Spanish scientists reported that in the sexual thrashing of tentacles the squid would sometimes inadvertently inject its sperm packet into its own body, impregnating itself instead of its partner. Lily went to bed still laughing too hard to stop, and in the morning the staff found her dead but still smiling. She left her Mongolian chest to Chelsea.

Herbert Christmas went away to take a course on the pastoral care of the elderly and settled back into Goldengroves to serve his Lord. Twice a year he took a monastery weekend to keep himself focused, and though still appreciative of good eating he stopped fixating on food and became rather slim. Now and then, however, after ministering to Leonie, he required donuts.

Chelsea Dean went to graduate school in Anthropology but did not entirely desert her first major. She wrote a controversial monograph in which she argued that the quirks and habits of Special Education children should be approached from an anthropological point of view, that they would be better served by educators who recognized them as an exotic and somewhat savage tribe with its own folkways. For this she has taken a good deal of academic abuse. She does not give a rat's ass.

ANN TRACY, born in rural Maine early in 1941, reports that like other War Babies she has never been quite able to shake the conviction that if you don't buy a thing when you see it, it'll be gone when you turn around. This is perhaps pertinent as well to memories and writing. She grew up in the pleasantly intense world of the rural co-ed boarding school of which her father was head and at which her mother sometimes taught Latin. A brother, later, grew to be an anthropologist and collector. Ann, who loved it all, after graduate school taught and wrote at SUNY Plattsburgh.